EFFECTIVE ADVOCACY

EFFECTIVE ADVOCACY

BY

NOEL SHAW

First Edition

SWEET & MAXWELL

THOMSON REUTERS

Reprinted 2010

Published in 1996 by Thomson Reuters (Legal) Limited
(Registered in England & Wales, Company No 1679046. Registered Office
and address for service: 100 Avenue Road, London, NW3 3PF)
trading as Sweet & Maxwell

Printed and bound by CPI Antony Rowe, Chippenham, Wiltshire

For further information on our products and services, visit
www.sweetandmaxwell.co.uk

ISBN: 978 0421 56650 7

A CIP Catalogue record
for this book is available
from the British Library

To my pupilmaster
JACK A. DENBIN

and my pupilmistress
ALISON ARMOUR

in gratitude

CONTENTS

PREFACE

This book has two aims.

To include in one short, well-indexed volume information on evidential and procedural matters for easy reference in court.

Secondly, to provide cookbook versions ("follow the recipe faithfully for perfect results every time") of the main advocacy tasks.

I have taken particular care with the index, and in the glossary I have attempted to include every term one is likely to encounter in the lower courts. I will be very grateful to receive any feedback as to anything which has been omitted; anything which should have been omitted; and anything unhelpful or ambiguous.

In particular I owe a great debt of gratitude to stipendiary magistrate Mr Jeremy Connor of Bow Street Magistrates' Court for his enthusiasm and promptitude in reading the book in manuscript; and for the many helpful suggestions he made.

Noel Shaw
London
February 1996

INTRODUCTION

One's first few months in court are inevitably something of a baptism of
fire, however good the advocacy training one has had. The skills which
have to be mastered differ considerably, and some are, paradoxically,
more difficult in short cases than in big ones. Any complex case yields a
great deal of material requiring cross-examination, and time in which to
formulate a plan of attack. But it is difficult to prevent cross-examination
in a half-hour motor vehicle interference trial degenerating into " 'Oh no
I didn't', 'Oh yes you did' ".

The biggest difficulty is that all these skills have to be mastered at the
same time, rather like learning to drive. It is no more safe to ignore
hearsay while concentrating on cross-examination than it is to ignore
steering while learning gear-changing.

As if these were not problems enough, there are numerous aspects
of courtroom procedure which soon become second-nature, but are
bewildering at first; and there is an extensive range of procedural terms
to take one by surprise.

It is hoped this book will be of assistance both in court and in
preparation.

Outside Court

The five trial skills which cause the most difficulty are:
- avoiding leading questions
- detecting hearsay
- cross-examination
- objecting to evidence under PACE; and
- making speeches.

The approaches to each skill demonstrated in this book may not
produce great advocacy, but they will accomplish their purposes efficiently
and ethically.

Each type of trial – defence, prosecution and civil – is dealt with in a
separate chapter, for three reasons.

In advocacy training generally, each training session or exercise focuses
on one trial skill in isolation. This layout redresses the imbalance by
considering each skill as part of an overall trial strategy – the approach
required in court.

Secondly, each skill is considered in the contexts of different types of case. Cross-examination on behalf of the defence, for example, is very different from cross-examination on behalf of the prosecution. Duplication has been avoided by cross-referencing.

Thirdly, because every stage of each type of trial is dealt with, certain tasks on which it is rare to see written advice (such as how to edit an interview) are included.

In court

Features intended for use in court include:

Working Plans for bail applications, pleas in mitigation, speeches, submissions of various sorts including objections to evidence under PACE. These can be adapted and used while you develop your own style.

The remands flow-diagram indicates the stage a case has reached and refers you to an Outline of the procedure at the hearing.

Checklists to ensure your preparation for a bail application is complete.

Modes of address tables for ready reference.

The order of trial tables show at a glance the order in which evidence is given; the order of cross-examination; and how the order in which speeches are made depends upon what evidence is called.

The step-by-step guide to hearsay summarises the principles for use in court.

The glossary and index have been designed to enable you to find the information you need quickly.

Various of the tables and guides intended for use in court have been put together in Chapter 1, which is intended mainly for reference. Chapters 2–5 are each self-contained and may be read in any order.

EVIDENCE AND PROCEDURE

LEADING AND NOT LEADING

A leading question is traditionally defined as one which suggests its own answer.

Examples:
"You saw a fight in the 'Three Bells' pub on the 11th October, didn't you?"
"Was your house burgled on the 8th May?"

Although these questions are certainly leading, a more useful definition may be:

A leading question gives evidence
The test of whether a question is leading is whether evidence comes from the advocate. It is usually impossible to tell from the form of a question whether or not it leads.

Examples:
"What colour dress was she wearing?"
"What is the index number of your car?"

These may be, but are not necessarily, leading.

Example 1(a):
A.   I saw Amanda Pearson at the bus stop.
Q.   What colour dress was she wearing?

The question is leading: the advocate gives the evidence that Amanda Pearson was wearing a dress.

Example 1(b):
A.   My cousin came to the party in a new dress.
Q.   What colour dress was she wearing?

This is a non-leading question: it gives no information.

Example 2(a):
A.   I drove down Enderby Way.
Q.   What is the index number of your car?

The advocate's question tells the court nothing: it is not leading.

Example 2(b):
A.   I set out to deliver the presents to my sister-in-law.
Q.   What is the index number of your car?

By giving the evidence that the witness had a car, the advocate leads.

The Prohibition on Leading

By asking leading questions an advocate gives evidence. This has advantages and disadvantages.

It enables the evidence to be established quickly, clearly and surely. But it precludes any opportunity of assessing the witness's credibility. Both leading and non-leading questions are useful in examination-in-chief.

In the typical examination-in-chief the advocate uses leading questions to set the scene; then elicits the narrative part of the evidence without leading; and finally leads on any remaining undisputed matters.

How much of the evidence is in issue is always the decision of the opposing advocate. The rule is that in examination-in-chief and re-examination you must not lead any part of the evidence unless your opponent has given permission. It is a good habit never to ask a leading question, no matter how obvious it is that the matter is not in dispute, without seeking your opponent's leave, and acknowledging to the court that it has been given.

Example:
"Leading with permission, ma'am; isn't it right, Mr Dawkins, that on Tuesday, 9th December last year..."

If your opponent will not allow you to lead at all, you have to find a way of getting your witness started on her/his evidence. This is dealt with at pages 77–80.

Once the witness has begun, simply take care not to assume any fact until the witness has given evidence of it.

Example:
Instead of:
"When you came back from the shops, did you have fish fingers for tea?"
Ask:
Q.   When you finished shopping, did you return home or go somewhere else?

Q. When did you next eat?
Q. What did you eat?

The easiest way to ensure that all your questions are acceptable is to keep them short. Two types of question are mainly used in the non-leading parts of examination-in-chief.

A prodding question invites the witness to continue; it is absolutely non-leading

Examples:
"And then what happened?"
"Please continue."
"Yes?"

Prodding questions allow you to control the speed at which the evidence is given, but because they give you no control over its content, they should be used only when you are confident the witness will give the evidence you want.

A prompting question suggests the category of answer; it narrows the field of responses

Examples:
"Where did you go?"
   (Suggested category: places)
"Did you notice anything about the vehicle?"
   (Suggested category: appearance of vehicle)
"What was the very next thing you did?"
   (Suggested category: an action immediately following the last thing mentioned)

A prompting question is non-leading only if every assumption has been established in evidence by the witness.

Example:
"How did you travel to work on the 24th June?"

This question is leading unless there has been evidence to support its underlying assumptions:

Q. Are you presently in work or not in work?
Q. Which days of the week do you work?
Q. When did you begin that job?
Q. Always working the same days per week?
Q. Did you work [ ]day the 24th June?
Q. How did you travel to work on that day?

Prompting questions are not objectionable as leading, but they retain substantial control over the witness. A particularly useful variety of prompting question is the forced-choice question.

Example:
"When you finished shopping did you return home or go somewhere else?"

Because the question covers every possibility (the witness, after shopping, must have gone somewhere) and does not direct the witness to either (or any) particular answer, the evidence comes from the witness and the question is not leading.

Leading, prompting and prodding questions all have their place in examination-in-chief: whenever you are confident the witness is giving the evidence you want, only prod.

If your opponent agrees there is no dispute on a part of the evidence, only lead.

If you have to establish the evidence from the witness, ask only short questions, taking care not to assume any fact the witness has not stated.

Cross-Examination

There is no prohibition on leading questions in cross-examination and they are frequently used, especially in putting one's case to a witness.

Example:
Q. There were only four, weren't there?
A. No, there were five.
Q. And they were at least fifty metres away, weren't they?
A. Not so far as that.

Nevertheless, if you expect a favourable answer it is better not to lead as the evidence will have more impact if it comes from the witness than from you.

HEARSAY

Hearsay is the category of evidence which causes the most difficulty to newly-qualified advocates who are often unsure whether evidence is hearsay at all and, if so, whether it is admissible under an exception to the rule.

The following is a severely practical, non-academic approach.

1. Be mindful of all reported speech in witness statements

Example:
"A shopper told us the boys we were chasing had gone down Hathaway Street" is as much reported speech as:
"A shopper said to me: 'The boys you are chasing went that way', pointing down Hathaway Street".

2. The words of your client may be excluded under PACE, but they will not be excluded as hearsay

3. The words of your client's co-defendant should be excluded, unless they are a confession by her/him (They are never evidence against your client.)

Example I:
"Johnny and I stole the money"

"I stole the money" is admissible against the co-defendant as a confession. It is only fair to put in his full statement or it may seem as though he accepts the entire blame, so the whole statement is admissible as a confession.

It is not evidence against Johnny (but he is unlikely to derive much comfort from that).

Example II:
"It wasn't me, it was Johnny"

"It wasn't me" is admissible against the co-defendant as evidence of reaction to accusation. "It was Johnny" is inadmissible as hearsay, unless Johnny "adopted" it. (This is unlikely and you should always resist any attempt to admit evidence under this exception to the hearsay rule. For a defendant to "adopt" by silence words of accusation, they must be spoken in her/his presence by someone on equal terms with her/him, in circumstances in which it would be reasonable to expect a response. You will not encounter this exception in your first cases.)

4A. In considering speech by someone who is not a defendant, first ask: Is the speech factual?

Speech which is genuinely non-factual is admissible. It is not hearsay.

Example I:
"I rang the bell. A man answered the door and said, 'Come in'."

"Come in" is an invitation or order; it is not "factual". The witness could give evidence that s/he was invited into the house, and s/he can give evidence the householder said, "Come in". The witness knows, of her/his own direct knowledge, that s/he was invited into the house.

Example II:
"Several people who were gathered round were shouting 'Hit him!' and 'Do him!'."

"Hit him!" is an exhortation, order or invitation; it is not factual. The witness knows of her/his own direct knowledge that the people were egging someone on to attack someone.

Example III:
"As I went down the road, a man asked, 'Can you direct me to the station?'"

This is a question. It may be seeking facts, but is not itself factual. It is not hearsay.

4B. It is important to beware of disguised factual statements

Example I:
"We chased the suspect to the junction. A woman on the corner said, 'Go down there'. We ran down Green Lane where we saw, and arrested, the defendant."

"Go down there" has the form of an order or exhortation. In this example the words either effectively mean "He went down there" or they are irrelevant. They are a factual statement in the form of an order. They are inadmissible as hearsay.

Example II:
"I asked his girlfriend if the defendant was at home. She replied, 'Do you want to buy drugs?'"

The words have the form of a question, but their only relevance is the implication that the defendant sells drugs. They are a disguised factual statement. They are inadmissible as hearsay.

5. In considering a factual statement by someone who is not a defendant, first ask: For what reason is the statement included in the evidence?

If the only reason for including the statement is as evidence of the facts it asserts, it is inadmissible as hearsay.

If there is a different reason for including the statement, it will usually be admissible for that purpose. Statements may be admitted to prove the listener's state of mind (only if relevant); the time when the statement was made; the state of mind of the maker (if relevant); or to prove anything else of relevance except the facts the statement asserts.

Example I:
"The store detective told me a youth in a tee-shirt with the slogan

'Mabel's brasserie' had just stolen a pair of jeans. I chased a man I now know to be the defendant, who was wearing such a tee-shirt, and called, 'Stop!'. He kept on running. I placed my hand on his arm and he hit me in the mouth."

The store detective's words are not spoken by a defendant. They are factual. If offered as evidence of the facts they assert (that the youth stole the jeans) they are inadmissible as hearsay.

If they are offered to prove what the police officer believed they are admissible if his state of mind is relevant.

So, if the only charge is shop-lifting they are inadmissible as hearsay. If there is also a charge of assault on a constable in the execution of his duty, they are admissible to prove the constable had reason to stop the youth and was therefore acting in the execution of his duty (which must be proved) when the youth assaulted him.

Example II:

The male householder of 52, The Larches, has given evidence that the burglary was discovered at about 6.30 p.m.
The female householder of the same address has given evidence the burglary was discovered about 5.30 p.m.
The police evidence is: "At 5.32 p.m. we received information of a burglary at 52, The Larches".

If the police evidence stood alone, it must be being offered as evidence of the facts it asserts (that there had been a burglary at 52, The Larches). It would be inadmissible as hearsay.

In this case, the timing of the discovery of the burglary is important. The purpose of the police evidence is to prove the accuracy of the time given by the female householder. The police evidence is admissible to corroborate the female householder's evidence in that regard.

Example III:

"I heard cries of 'Help! Help!', coming from the shop, so I ran inside and saw a man and a woman."

"Help! Help!" is not a factual statement and, so far as one can tell from this short extract, is not a disguised factual statement. It is admissible as evidence of what the witness her/himself directly saw and heard: the question of hearsay does not arise.

6. Evidence that someone (always a police officer) did something because of a conversation is always inadmissible, even when the words of the conversation are not given

This essentially dishonest device invites the tribunal to imagine a conversation of which no evidence is given. You should always object.

Example I:

"I saw a Ford car index P987 QRS with its tyres slashed. A woman nearby said something to me. As a result of what she said, I went over to a youth, who I now know to be the defendant..."

Test it this way. Compare the above extract with this:

"I saw a Ford car index P987 QRS with its tyres slashed. I went over to a youth nearby, who I now know to be the defendant..."

The first extract implies that the woman linked the defendant to the damaged car. It is an implied factual statement offered as evidence of the facts it asserts. It is inadmissible as hearsay. The evidence should be given as in the second extract.

Example II:

A statement of PC Kelly is read section 9, in which he says he saw a car (he does not give the number) commit a traffic offence.

PC Stretch: "I spoke on my personal radio to PC Kelly."
Q: "Do not tell us what he said, but as a result of it, did you do something?"
PC Stretch: "Yes, I stopped car index L642 FDB and spoke to the driver who I now know to be the defendant."

There is a continuity problem here (usually the PC who sees the offence walks up to the car which has been stopped further on by another PC). The prosecutor and PC Stretch are attempting to plug the gap by implying PC Kelly told PC Stretch to stop the car he in fact stopped.

Object to this evidence as inadmissible hearsay. At half-time, submit there is no evidence linking the offending car with your client's car. If you are over-ruled, appeal the conviction by way of case stated.

Example III:

"As a result of a message on my personal radio I went to 19, Pontbeck House, Cumberland Avenue."

There is nothing here to indicate that the "message" was not an order from a superior officer. The only objection to the officer stating s/he went to the address on the orders of her/his superior officer is on the ground of relevance (it does not matter why s/he went, so long as s/he went). There is no question of hearsay.

Example IV:

"Acting on information received I went to 19, Pontbeck House, Cumberland Avenue."

If the evidence as a whole suggests what the information was, it is inadmissible as hearsay (as it is offered as evidence of the facts it asserts).

If there is no indication what the "information received" was, there is no hearsay; but the formula is undesirable as it implies there is more evidence than is called, and should be avoided.

7. **Hearsay in documents is too large a subject for this step-by-step guide. Sections 23–26 of the Criminal Justice Act 1988 are well worth learning thoroughly. As a rule of thumb, in criminal proceedings "official" documents in road traffic cases are generally admissible under specific statutory provisions. Otherwise, apart from section 9 statements, written factual statements offered as evidence of the facts they assert are inadmissible as hearsay**

Example:
A motorist is being prosecuted for driving a car fitted with tyres unsuitable for road use. The tyres in question are heavily stamped: "Unsuitable for road use".

The motorist must be acquitted unless the stopping police officer or another witness can give expert evidence of the tyres' unsuitability. Evidence of the words on the tyres is inadmissible as hearsay (*Patel v. Comptroller of Customs* [1966] A.C. 356).

RES GESTAE

Only a small percentage of practising advocates are confident of being able to define the doctrine of *res gestae* accurately and comprehensively.

Pace, and with respect to, Sir Rupert Cross, the doctrine is most conveniently thought of as two exceptions to the rule against hearsay.

1. Statements about matters only the speaker can know about her/himself

Examples:
"I have a pain in my stomach"
"I am baking this cake for Ali's birthday"
"I intend to go to Scotland next week"
"I am a Conservative"

A witness can give evidence of what a non-witness said contemporaneously about bodily sensation, including illness; intention; opinions; and the reason for an act. Only statements about illness are likely to occur more than very seldom.

Example I:

The prosecutor proposes to read section 9 a doctor's statement in which the doctor recounts the symptoms described by the victim of an assault.

Defence: My friend cannot read what the victim said to the doctor because that is hearsay.

Pros: My friend is, of course, right that it is hearsay, but is it admissible under the rule in *Nicholas* (1846) 2 Car & Kir 246. At page 248 the learned Chief Baron held: "If a man says to his surgeon, 'I have a pain in the head' or in such a part of the body, that is evidence".

Example II:

The defendant has claimed in mitigation that she drove when uninsured only because her brother had become unwell and she had taken over the driving.

    A prosecution witness can give evidence that he had asked the brother: "Are you alright?", and he had replied, "Yeah, I'm fine".

2. Spontaneous statements made contemporaneously with exciting events, where there is no possibility of concoction

It is safe to say that you will not have to concern yourself with this second category of *res gestae* in your first few months' practice.

    Virtually all authority on it derives from murder cases, and there can be very few other cases in which this exception will arise. A witness can give evidence of the statement of a participant in, or observer of, an event if the statement was made approximately contemporaneously; the event was such as to dominate the person's mind; and the court is satisfied there is no possibility the statement was concocted by the participant or observer.

    As there is authority (*R v. Andrews* [1987] 1 All E.R. 513, 521) that statements should not be admitted under this exception where it is possible to call the participant or observer, it can be seen that the exception is not often relied on; and, in relatively simple cases in the magistrates' courts, virtually never.

PRODUCING EXHIBITS

If you have time (the police often attend court very late) check that each exhibit is what it should be; that it is labelled; and which officer seized it.

    Take all the exhibits into court with you. At the point in the witness's evidence where s/he mentions the object, pass the exhibit to her/him and ask her/him to identify it; then assign it an exhibit number.

Example:

A.   I saw the defendant drop the screwdriver onto the footway and walk away from the car. I picked up the screwdriver, and went up to the defendant.

Q.   Let me pass you this [hands screwdriver to usher]. Is that the screwdriver you picked up?

A.   It is.

Q.   May this be "Exhibit 1", sir?

Bench: Certainly.

Q.   You went up to the defendant, you say?

A.   Yes. I said to him...

Do not ask the witness how s/he can identify the object or whether s/he is sure it is the correct object. These are matters for re-examination if challenged in cross-examination.

The question identifying the object ("Is this the screwdriver?") is, of course, leading. But both parties are aware that the exhibit was handed to the advocate by the witness (or, in the case of police witnesses, by the exhibits officer) immediately before the trial, so there is an appearance of leading rather than reality.

The usual system of labelling is to call the first exhibit "Exhibit 1", and so on. If you produce the first exhibit, suggest it be labelled in this way. The court may indicate it uses some other system, for example, Joan Smith's first exhibit is "JS1".

Producing Photographs

The admissibility of a photograph is never a problem. It can be produced in evidence by anyone who can identify its subject matter (*Tolson* (1864) 4 F & F 103).

Thus a witness can produce a photograph of her/himself to show injuries. The owner of a car can produce a photograph if s/he has compared the photograph with the car.

There is never an absolute need to call the photographer with regard to admissibility. It may be beneficial to call her/him with regard to weight.

If a party produces a photograph alleged to be of the road on which an accident occurred, and the other party disputes it was the road in question, or states that the photograph has been taken from such a vantage-point and with such a lens as to give a misleading impression, then although the photograph can be admitted, little weight may be attached to it unless the photographer is called to say precisely where and with what lens it was taken.

Sketches

Any witness may give evidence by means of a sketch. If the sketch has been produced before the witness came into court s/he should give evidence that s/he prepared it earlier. Its accuracy may be disputed, like any of the witness's other evidence.

Maps, Plans

It is often useful to have a plan before the court. If the parties are agreed that it can be used it need not be produced as evidence, and it is not evidence. It is merely an aid to understanding the evidence.

You can refer to a map as of right, without the agreement of the other side, if it is accepted by the court as a work of reference. You will never have any difficulty in relying on an A – Z or Ordnance Survey map.

MODES OF ADDRESS

Court	Addressing	Referring to
Magistrates' court; Youth court	Sir/Madam	The court
Crown Court Except:—High Court judges; all judges at the Old Bailey; and the Recorders of Manchester and Liverpool, all of whom are addressed as High Court judges	Your Honour	His/her Honour
High Court	My Lord/Lady	His Lordship/Ladyship
County Court District Judge	Sir/Madam	The learned district judge
Circuit Judge	Your Honour	His/her Honour

Magistrates' Courts/Youth Courts

Unless one of the wing persons asks you a question, address only the chair(wo)man but make eye-contact with all three. If you are asked a question by the clerk, address your answer to the chair(wo)man. Thus if the clerk is male and the chairwoman female, address your reply to "ma'am". Refer to the wing members as "your colleagues".

> *Example:*
> "I do not know whether you or your colleagues are familiar with that road, ma'am?"

"Madam" may be pronounced as it looks, or as "mam" ("marm", like "M'lud", has gone out of fashion).

The Crown Court

High Court judges and the Recorders of Liverpool and Manchester, wherever they are sitting and whatever case they are trying, are always addressed as High Court judges (see below).

Anyone sitting as a judge at the Old Bailey is addressed as a High Court judge (see below).

Anyone else sitting as a Crown Court judge is addressed as "Your Honour". In addressing the judge the invariable form is "Your Honour". In referring to the judge, you may use "Her/His Honour the Judge" or merely "Her/His Honour".

> *Examples:*
> "Your Honour, there is a matter of law..."
> "May it please Your Honour, I appear..."
> "Tell His Honour where you left the car"
> "Subject to any directions Her Honour the Judge gives you, ladies and gentlemen..."

"May it please you, Your Honour" is correct but repetitious. "May it please Your Honour" is better.

The High Court

Three forms of reference and address must be differentiated:

(I) Directly addressing the judge

This is the equivalent of "sir" in the magistrates' court, or a personal name. The only form to use in direct address is "My Lady/My Lord".

Examples:
"Have you got a light, George?"
"Can I assist you further, ma'am?"
"I appear for the applicant, My Lady"
"A PSR has been prepared, My Lord"

(II) Referring to the judge when addressing her/him

This is the equivalent of "you", "to you", "before you", "next to you", etc. It is never the equivalent of a personal name. The only form to use is "Your Ladyship/Your Lordship".

Examples:
"Have you got a light?"
"Can I assist you further?"
"Has Your Ladyship got a light?"
"Can I assist Your Lordship further?"
"May I hand this up to Your Lordship?"
"The matter before Your Ladyship is..."

(III) Referring to the judge, when addressing someone else

Two forms can be used: "Her Ladyship/His Lordship" or "My Lord/My Lady".

Examples:
"Tell My Lady where you left the car"
"Tell Her Ladyship when you entered the house"
"Direct your answers to His Lordship"
"Subject to any directions My Lord gives you, ladies and gentlemen..."

It is worth spending some time becoming quite clear about these three forms. A common mistake is to use "Your Ladyship/Your Lordship" when directly addressing the judge. This is always wrong.

Example:
It is always incorrect to say:
"I appear for the prosecution, Your Lordship"
or:
"Your Ladyship, a PSR has been prepared"

The rule is that the only form of direct address (the equivalent of "madam" or "mate") is "My Lady/My Lord". "May it please you, My Lady" is not incorrect, but "May it please Your Ladyship" is better.

Civil Cases

A District Judge is addressed as "Madam/Sir".

A High Court judge is invariably addressed as "My Lord/My Lady", wherever s/he is sitting. Anyone sitting in the High Court is addressed as "My Lady/My Lord", whoever s/he is.

A Circuit Judge trying a High Court case is addressed as "My Lady/My Lord" wherever s/he is sitting. S/he is otherwise addressed as "Your Honour".

If your sentences are becoming heavy with "Your Honours", slip in a few "you's". In time you will instinctively phrase your sentences to avoid the problem.

Example:
Rather than say:

"This matter was last before Your Honour on the 23rd April when Your Honour ordered a pre-sentence report, and reserved the matter to Your Honour. Your Honour will recall that this offence took place on..."

say:

"This matter was last before Your Honour on the 23rd April when Your Honour ordered a pre-sentence report and reserved the matter to yourself. Your Honour will recall..."

or:

"On 23rd April Your Honour ordered a pre-sentence report in this matter and reserved it to yourself. Your Honour will recall..."

The Clerk

The clerk in any court is addressed as "Madam (or Mr) Clerk", and referred to (in addressing the court) as "your learned clerk" or (in addressing anyone else) "the learned clerk".

Other Advocates

Other advocates are referred to as "my friend" or "m'learned friend". If there are more than two advocates in the case they can be distinguished as "m'friend for the second defendant", "m'friend for the prosecution", "m'learned friend Ms Shah", etc.

THE ORDER OF A CRIMINAL TRIAL

Prosecution opening
Prosecution evidence-in-chief
    —cross-examination on behalf of the First Defendant
    —cross-examination on behalf of the Second (Third, *etc.*,) Defendant
    —re-examination
First Defendant's opening, (see (1) below)
First Defendant's evidence-in-chief
    —cross-examination on behalf of Second Defendant
    —cross-examination on behalf of Third (Fourth, *etc.*,) Defendant
    —cross-examination on behalf of prosecution
    —re-examination
First Defendant's first (Second, *etc.*,) witness's evidence-in-chief
    —cross-examination on behalf of Second (Third, *etc.*,) Defendant
    —cross-examination on behalf of prosecution
    —re-examination
Second Defendant's (Third, *etc.*,) evidence-in-chief..., *etc.*,
Prosecution closing speech, (see (2) below)
First Defendant's (Second, *etc.*,) closing speech

(1) In the Crown Court a defence advocate makes an opening speech only if s/he calls at least one witness apart from the defendant and character witnesses; in the magistrates' court, only instead of making a closing speech

(2) In the Crown Court the prosecutor makes a closing speech only if the defence have called at least one witness to fact; in the magistrates' court no prosecution closing speech is made

THE ORDER OF A CIVIL TRIAL

The judge may give directions as to the order of the trial (C.C.R. 1981, Ord. 21, r. 5A). The usual order depends upon whether the defendant calls evidence. It is either:

Plaintiff's opening
Plaintiff's evidence-in-chief, (see (1) below)
    —cross-examination on behalf of the First Defendant
    —cross-examination on behalf of the Second (Third, *etc.*,) Defendant
    —re-examination
First Defendant's evidence-in-chief, (see (1) below)
    —cross-examination on behalf of Second (Third, *etc.*,) Defendant
    —cross-examination on behalf of Plaintiff

—re-examination
Second (Third, *etc.*,) Defendant's evidence-in-chief (see (1) below), . . .*etc.*,
First Defendant's closing speech, (see (2) below)
Second (Third, *etc.*,) Defendant's closing speech
Plaintiff's closing speech

(1) A party who testifies may do so at any convenient point in the order of the evidence called on her/his behalf (unlike the defendant to a criminal charge who, if s/he gives evidence, generally must do so before calling any other witness)

(2) The usual practice is that only one speech is made on behalf of a defendant which is generally a closing speech

OR:

Plaintiff's opening
Plaintiff's evidence-in-chief
  —cross-examination on behalf of the First Defendant
  —cross-examination on behalf of the Second (Third, *etc.*,) Defendant
  —re-examination
Plaintiff's closing speech
First Defendant's closing speech
Second (Third, *etc.*,) Defendant's closing speech

CHAPTER 2

CRIMINAL TRIAL—DEFENCE

PREPARATION

Do You Need More Time?

The following guide assumes you have been sent at the last minute and received no instructions until you met your client outside court: the conditions under which many advocates undertake their first trials.

The first thing to do is check with the usher or list-caller how much time you have before your case will be called on. If you will need more time than that, let the usher know at once so s/he can do her/his best to accommodate you. If this is not possible, explain briefly to the court that you have been instructed late, and need time with the client to take her/his instructions. If the court is reluctant to give you more time, point out that time spent in preparation invariably saves time in the conduct of the case. It is also sensible to ask in court for the prosecution to give you copies of any witness statements you do not already have, as this will save further time.

Remember that for all but those with the most extensive records, a criminal conviction is always a very serious matter, and it would be quite wrong to represent anyone, inadequately prepared.

Meeting the Client

No matter how great a rush you are in, always spend two or three minutes reassuring your client and explaining the court procedure. Being tried for a criminal offence is a traumatic experience and work with your client will go much more smoothly if you take a little time to establish a working relationship at the outset.

Politely but firmly discourage her/him from giving you her/his account of what happened. Explain that it is necessary for you to be quite directive to make best use of the limited time available. Tell your client that immediately before going into court you will explain the court procedure to her/him. Then tell the client that you must have some time (depending on the length of the witness statements) to consider the case against her/him.

If s/he is accompanied by friends or relatives, ask your client whether s/he may want to call any of them as witnesses. If so, politely but firmly explain to any potential witnesses that you cannot take your client's instructions in their presence, and make arrangements to see them to take their proofs of evidence later on.

Even if the friends or relatives are not potential witnesses, it will often be easier to take instructions from your client alone. Unless your client is a young person accompanied by a parent or other adult, it may be wise to suggest at the beginning that you speak to her/him alone, and only invite the friends or relatives to join you after you have taken instructions.

No Prosecution Witness Statements

If you do not already have them, ask the prosecutor for copies of the prosecution witness statements. If s/he is reluctant to provide them, there are various arguments which may assist. If the charges are either-way and the statements have been served and lost, it can hardly be right that that should disadvantage the defendant.

If the charges are summary and involve significant civilian evidence, the defendant will usually have been interviewed (except in a road traffic case) and a summary of the interview will have been served. You are entitled to hear the tape (which is potentially an exhibit) which will usually reveal the substance of the allegations. The threat of an adjournment in the middle of the case while the defence listen to the tape will persuade most prosecutors to disclose the witness statements.

If all the evidence is from police officers you can point out that you are entitled to inspect the notebooks and it will save time in court if you can either inspect them now, or have statements.

If you do not see the prosecution evidence in advance, make sure it is given slowly enough for you to take full notes, and go through them with your client (as at pages 23–24 below) before you cross-examine.

Indicate only once to the court that the reason the case is going so slowly is that you have not been shown the witness statements ("even though it is a very simple case" or "even though the evidence is relatively complex" as appropriate), and *take as much time as you need.*

Do not agree that any witness statements can be read section 9 until you have had an opportunity to consider the case as a whole.

PROSECUTION WITNESS STATEMENTS

With experience, you will automatically note certain aspects of the prosecution case which often determine the shape of the defence; you can ensure you do not overlook these aspects in your first few months by applying the "Four F's" filter to the prosecution evidence.

Full?

Is there some evidence on each element of each offence? Before you look at any of the prosecution statements look up each of the offences your client is charged with in Anthony & Berryman, Archbold, or Blackstone's. Write out a list of the elements.

Example:
Shoplifting

—dishonestly
—appropriates
—property
—belonging to another
—with the intention permanently to deprive

As you copy out the list of elements, be mindful of terms of legal art—such as "dishonestly" or "intending"—and put a question-mark against any of whose meaning you are not sure.

Never skimp this task: it is fundamental to presenting your case. Then turn to the statements. Read each one with great concentration: do not skip from one to another. Against your list of elements of the offence, jot down the prosecution case and the evidence for it.

Example:

Element:	Facts:	Evidence:
dishonestly		inference
appropriates	Tuesday 19th March at Sainsbury's, puts into shopping-bag	seen by store detective
property	1) jar of coffee 2) fish fingers	seen by store detective found when searched
belonging to another	Sainsbury's	loser's statement
with the intention permanently to deprive		inference

As you read each statement highlight in different colours (i) passages helpful to the defence, (ii) passages which cause difficulties to the defence, and (iii) inadmissible passages (such as hearsay). In the margin indicate parts of the statement you need to ask your client about. Check that there is some evidence on each of the elements you have listed.

Example:
Public Order Act 1986, s. 4
The defendant is alleged to have shouted: "Tomorrow you'll be dead meat."

There is no evidence the defendant threatened immediate violence. If evidence on one element is missing, it is likely you will make a half-time submission in respect of that charge (see pages 51 and 61–62). If there is an absence of evidence on one element or there is a problem with part of the evidence, note that in a fourth column of your elements/evidence table.

Example:

Element:	Facts:	Evidence:	Problems:
dishonestly		inference	
appropriates	puts into shopping-bag	seen by store detective	
property	1) coffee 2) fish fingers	" found when searched	
belonging to another	Sainsbury's		No evi fish fingers from Sainsbury's

Fair?

Would the admission of any of the evidence be so unfair that it ought not to be admitted?

If your client is alleged to have made any admissions, consider carefully the circumstances in which s/he made them. Were paragraphs 10–12 of Code C complied with? If there were breaches of the Code, and the only evidence on one element (intention, for example) is a confession, it is likely you will seek to exclude the confession at half-time (see pages 45–50), and then make a submission of No Case.

If the exclusion of the confession would still leave a case to answer, you will need to have two plans for the defence case to allow for whether or not the confession is excluded.

Fingered?

How is your client identified? The usual means are: arrest at the scene; identification by a witness (maybe the complainant) who knows the defendant well; fingerprint evidence; or an admission of presence in interview.

If you can exclude one link in the chain of identification evidence there will be no *prima facie* case against your client and at the close of the prosecution case you will be able to make a submission.

If identification is by admission in interview, consider whether the interview was conducted fairly and in compliance with Code C.

If identification is by witnesses picking out suspects (at an ID parade, or by driving past suspects in the street, or however), consider the evidence carefully, as you may have to submit that the procedure was such that the admission of that evidence would have so adverse an effect on the fairness of the proceedings that the evidence ought not to be admitted (see pages 47–49).

If identification is by fingerprints, check the continuity of both sets of prints carefully.

Check that no link in the identification chain is hearsay.

Example:
The defendant carelessly drives into Victim's car, and drives on without stopping. Bystander gives Victim a note of the defendant's number which is handed in to the police who serve on the registered keeper of the vehicle (who is, in fact, the defendant) a notice requiring him to name the driver at the time in question. The defendant returns the form naming himself as driver.

There is no case to answer unless Bystander is brought to court to give evidence of the number of the car involved in the accident.

Of course, even if the identification evidence is clearly admissible you may still have to challenge it in cross-examination and submit in closing that it is unsafe to found a conviction on (see page 60).

Facts

As a last resort you can fight the case on the facts.

TAKING A PROOF OF EVIDENCE

Begin by asking your client a question based on the prosecution statements to which you expect her/his reply to be "Yes".

Example:
"Were you in Clashfern Avenue on Tuesday 19th April at about 8 in the evening?"

Then ask her/him two or three questions to establish the context.

Example:
"Why were you there?"
"Where were you going to?"

Establish a little (only a little) non-contentious background material. Use the answers to begin the proof.

Example:
"Earlier this year I used to do a carpentry evening class every Tuesday at the Taylor Institute. It started about half-past six and went on until about 8 o'clock. I would then walk home with my friend Alan Bloggs who also went to the class. The Taylor Institute is in Griffiths Road, so to get to my home in Brandon Street, I would walk along Bridge Street to the end, turn left into Clashfern Avenue and go along it until I came to Templeman Avenue which I would turn into."

Take down your client's account of the incident, dealing with everything which s/he is said to have done or said.

Example:
Q: Is it right you were carrying a carrier bag?
A: Two, actually.
Q: Is it right you said 'Good evening' to the woman at number 71?
A: Yes.

might become:

"In my left hand I was holding two carrier bags, one containing my carpentry overalls and the other some tins of beer I had bought at the off-licence. As we passed Number 71 Clashfern Avenue I said 'Good evening' to Mrs Slynn who lives there."

As you are taking your client's proof, note any points which contradict the prosecution statements, or are not mentioned in them. Include them also in your table of evidence and elements of the offence.

Example:

Element:	Facts:	Evidence:	Problems:
dishonestly		inference	reaction inconsistent with dishonesty
appropriates	puts into shopping-bag	seen by store detective	did not look round then put coffee into bag—put it in by mistake
property	(1) coffee (2) fish fingers	found when searched	
belonging to another	Sainsbury's		no evi fish fingers from Sainsbury's

In addition to asking your client what s/he said and did at the time in question, find out what information s/he can give you about the evidence against her/him.

Examples:
Why would the complainant make an allegation against your client? Has there been a quarrel?
From where the witness claims to have been standing, would it be possible to see what s/he claims to have seen?

Do not include this information in your client's proof, but note the points in the margins of the relevant prosecution statements.

Example:
"Previous quarrel with client about parking spaces and loud music."

Taking Proofs of Witnesses' Evidence

Always see potential witnesses one by one, away from your client. Begin by asking a question to which you are very sure her/his answer will be "yes". Take especial care not to lead by suggesting an answer the witness might not otherwise have given.

Do not show her/him either the prosecution witness statements or your client's proof of evidence. If the potential witness asks you what your client has said about something, tell her/him that it is her/his account that you want. If the witness appears genuinely anxious that s/he may not remember the event accurately, you can tell her/him that everyone, including the court, realises that after several months there are bound to be inaccuracies and discrepancies.

Be completely neutral in taking the potential witness's proof. If it contradicts what your client has told you, that is something you will have to take up with your client, not with the potential witness. Ask her/him about all the matters in all the prosecution statements and in your client's proof of which you would expect this potential witness to have knowledge, but always taking care to do so in a non-leading way.

Example:
Instead of:
"Did you notice that the defendant was carrying two carrier bags?"
ask:
"Did you happen to notice whether or not the defendant was carrying anything?"

When you have taken the complete proof, explain the court procedure to the witness.

COURTROOM PROCEDURE

(1) Give the witness an estimate of the earliest time s/he may possibly be called (s/he may like to go and get a cup of tea).

(2) If the witness may feel uncomfortable sitting near the opposing party, ask the usher for a suitable place for her/him to sit.

(3) The witness must ensure the usher knows where s/he is.

(4) S/he must not discuss the evidence with any other potential witness.

(5) S/he must not go into court until called by the usher.

(6) S/he will be led up to the witness box and, if s/he has a religion, asked to take the holy book in her/his right hand and take the appropriate oath. Ask whether s/he is happy to do that.

(7) If s/he is not wearing her/his reading glasses the usher will read the oath for her/him to repeat.

(8) If s/he does not have a religion or does not wish to take an oath on the holy book (perhaps at a particular time), tell her/him to say to the usher that s/he wishes to affirm.

(9) You will then ask her/him questions. Although you are asking the questions s/he should face the magistrates and answer to them. S/he should make a deliberate effort to speak very loudly, and slowly enough for the evidence to be written down.

(10) The first questions will be the witness's name and address. If s/he is reluctant to give her/his address in open court, s/he should

write it on paper, and you will apply for it to be given by handing the paper to the clerk.

(11)   You are not allowed to suggest the answers to the witness, but you will broadly follow the sequence of the proof of evidence or statement so it is important that the witness reads it several times and is very familiar with it. If s/he discovers any mistakes in it, s/he should inform you or (in the case of a prosecution witness) a police officer.

(12)   The other advocate(s) will then ask her/him some questions. S/he should ignore the way in which the questions are asked, and simply think: what information is being asked for, and give it. If s/he cannot remember, that is what s/he should say.

(13)   S/he may be asked further questions by the magistrates or by you.

(14)   When s/he is "released" by the magistrates, s/he may either sit at the back of the court or leave.

(15)   Stress (i) that s/he should ignore the manner in which questions are asked and concentrate on answering accurately; (ii) that s/he should speak very loudly; (iii) and it will be very helpful if s/he will read through her/his proof of evidence several times before going into court and (if there is only one copy) on her/his way to the witness box will hand it to the usher to give to you.

PREPARING THE DEFENCE

The number of defences to any particular charge is very small. To the possession of drugs, one defence is that they may have belonged to another occupant of the premises; the other defence is plant. To shop-lifting, the only defence is mistake.

The defence case, therefore, will follow one of a very small number of patterns. Knowing only the charge her/his client faces, an experienced advocate on her/his way to court can anticipate the course of the trial and rehearse her/his closing speech. When s/he meets and takes instructions from the client it is merely a question of slotting the particular facts into the well-worn pattern of cases of its kind.

Example I:
Public Order Act 1986, s.5
The defendant is alleged to have been one of a group of youths shouting abuse at police officers.

The possible defences are that the words were not said, or were said but not by the defendant; or that the police would not be likely to be caused harassment, alarm or distress by those words. The two lines of defence can be run together.

One will therefore open up the possibility that the officers are mistaken as to what words were said, or who said them (distance, level of noise, number of people around, presence or absence of independent witnesses, whether the youths ran off).

Example II:
Actual Bodily Harm

The usual defence is self-defence, another is accident.

One will therefore bring out the complainant's motivation for attacking the defendant; one will explore the reasons why any witnesses tend to favour the complainant rather than the defendant; one will emphasize the inevitable discrepancies between the witnesses' accounts of the detail of what happened; and one will argue that the injuries are more consistent with the defendant's account.

Examining the Evidence

You now have the defence version of what happened and the prosecution version (or versions. The prosecutor will try to meld the evidence of the various witnesses into one coherent account. You should be alive to, and accentuate, any discrepancies).

If you had to decide between those versions, what questions would you ask, and what further information would you want?

Example:
"The defendant stopped, looked around furtively, picked up the jar of coffee, slipped it into his own shopping bag".

"I was walking down the aisle on my way to another section of the supermarket. I noticed the coffee which I had not been intending to buy and, without stopping, took a jar from the shelf and, by mistake, slipped it into my own bag instead of the wire basket."

—Was anyone else in the aisle who would have seen whether or not the defendant was standing or walking when he picked up the coffee?
—How was he holding his bag?
—What sort of bag was it?
—Where was the store detective?
—Would the store detective have been visible from where the defendant is said to have stood?
—Was a closed circuit TV system in operation?

—With what words was the defendant stopped by the store detective?

—What was his response to being stopped?

If the prosecution statements raise questions in your mind which your client cannot answer, it will usually be wise to obtain the answers from the witness via the prosecutor before the case begins, unless to do so may alert her/him to an aspect of the case better overlooked. Certainly you should only ask opposing witnesses questions in cross-examination to which you have little idea of the answers if you are quite sure you know what you are doing.

Be objective in considering the versions. Do not look only for evidence which weakens the prosecution case, but note each side's strong and weak points. Put the prosecution's weak points to your client. It may be that s/he, having been present at the incident, can clear up points which are obscure to you.

Put to your client the questions you would ask in cross-examination if you were prosecuting. This will prepare your client for the prosecution's questions (and you for your client's answers). Incorporate all the fresh information in the proof of evidence.

This consideration of the evidence from both points of view is the crucial part of your conduct of the case. Never do it less than thoroughly.

Your Argument

Your argument will generally follow one of two outlines: that part of the prosecution evidence is wrong (for example, it was the "Victim" who attacked the defendant) or, alternatively, is unreliable (one cannot be sure the witness has identified the right person). It is useful to have a provisional view of whether each witness is only unreliable or deliberately dishonest. As fully as you can, sketch in your argument.

Example I:
Public Order Act 1986, s.5

The defendant is alleged to have been one of the younger members of a group of about eight youths shouting racist abuse directed at one of two police officers who were on foot.

One will abandon the second-string argument that the officers would not have been caused harassment by the words.

The argument is that the officers could not be sure which of the youths shouted what; only a minority of the youths were caught; the officers are likely to have caught the slower youths, not necessarily the ones who shouted; the younger youths were slower. The defendants will give evidence they did not shout abuse. The court cannot be sure that they did.

Example II:
Actual Bodily Harm
The defendant is alleged to have begun punching the Victim after a quarrel arose about bumping into each other on a dance-floor.

The argument is that the "Victim" was quite drunk and punched the defendant who defended himself, the Victim being more seriously injured because the defendant is stronger. The only other witnesses are friends of the Victim who did not see the first blows, and who have been influenced by hearing the Victim's side of the story. In the absence of objective evidence such as security cameras, the court cannot be sure it was the defendant who attacked.

Your argument is the outline of your closing speech, subject to how the evidence emerges. It is the basis of your cross-examination. It is also the basis of your decisions about what evidence to call, and the linked question of whether your client may have to give evidence which may lead to her/his previous convictions being put to her/him.

YOUR CLIENT'S "SHIELD"

If your client gives evidence against a co-defendant, there is nothing you can do to prevent her/his advocate from cross-examining your client on her/his previous convictions, if relevant. Your client will therefore give such evidence only if strictly necessary to her/his defence.

If your client gives evidence of her/his own good character, that unnecessarily gives an opening for the prosecutor to apply to put in your client's previous convictions.

The greatest risk of your client losing her/his "shield" is where the defence involves imputations on the character of a prosecution witness or witnesses.

This difficult situation is exacerbated in the magistrates' court by the fact that the prosecutor's application to cross-examine itself makes the existence of a conviction known to the magistrates.

Stage 1: "Imputations on Character"

Decisions on what amounts to an imputation vary widely, and the facts of your client's case will not be the same as any decided case.

A useful rule of thumb is that if it is possible to regard the defence case as being that the witness is (however strangely) mistaken, there is no imputation; but if the defence is, in effect, that the witness has said what s/he knows is not true, that is an imputation.

The number of cases in which the defence necessarily involves alleging deliberate lies in now relatively small. The classic case was the alleged confession. Now that interviews in police stations are tape-recorded, there is never a challenge to the content of a long interview. Admissions alleged to have been made prior to formal interview can be challenged under PACE on the basis that the suspect should not have been questioned outside of formal interview conditions. If the words are ruled admissible, they can be challenged as mistaken recollection by the officer.

If your case falls into the small category in which witnesses must be accused of lying (for example, a defence of plant), it will usually be best for the defendant's convictions to be put in by the defence as part of its case at the first opportunity.

Examples:
"When you saw the defendant in Protheroe Street you were already aware he had drugs convictions, weren't you, officer?"

"If you are going to plant drugs on someone, you have to plant them on someone with drugs convictions, don't you, officer?"

The first question is a difficult one for the witness. If s/he says No, it may later be shown s/he was likely to have been aware of the convictions. If s/he says Yes, s/he appears to be making an admission, and that may throw her/him off-balance. If s/he hesitates, s/he may look dishonest.

The defence will then be seen by the tribunal as coming straight to the nub of the case: was this defendant, with admitted previous, fitted up by the police on this occasion? In much the more numerous category of cases, however, the defence can be put on the basis that the witness was mistaken.

Avoiding an Application
It may well be that if you explain to the prosecutor broadly what is challenged, and that the challenges are on the basis of mistake, not lies, s/he will agree that attempting to put in the defendant's previous is inappropriate. It may help to refer her/him to *Britzman* (see page 31).

If you do not wish to outline your case to the prosecutor, or s/he will not agree on the inappropriateness of the application, it will usually be possible to agree that if the prosecutor wants to make an application, s/he will ask the magistrates to withdraw so that the matter can be discussed with the clerk. If the prosecutor does not readily agree to this compromise, it may well be possible to enlist the help of the clerk in persuading her/him.

Stage 2: The Exercise of Discretion

If the prosecutor does make an application, you will argue that no imputation was made on the character of the prosecution witnesses and, alternatively, if such an imputation were made, the court should, in the exercise of its discretion, disallow cross-examination as to record.

Before making your submission, ask for the court's copy of *Britzman* [1983] 1 W.L.R. 350; [1983] 1 All E.R. 369; 76 Cr. App. R. 134.

It is the guideline case. It, in effect, endorses the principle in *Rouse* [1904] 1 K.B. 184 that a particular defendant's calling a witness a liar may be "nothing more than the traverse of the truth of an allegation" (and not an imputation). Secondly, it indicates that such cross-examination should be allowed only if the tribunal has to decide whether the prosecution witnesses have fabricated evidence. Thirdly, the case indicates the court should make allowance for the strain of being in the witness box, lack of education and the exaggerated use of language.

It will usually be of assistance to quote from that case. It will generally be wise to have as a sub-text the suggestion that the magistrates would prefer to decide the case on its merits rather than the defendant's record. Of course, this should never be directly stated.

Should Your Client Give Evidence?

The only obvious case in which you may advise your client not to give evidence is where identification is disputed and s/he has answered questions in interview and there is no alibi evidence. As it is her/his case s/he was not present at the incident, there is no useful evidence s/he can give in the witness box, and s/he has dealt with the case against her/him in interview.

In most other cases the defendant could give relevant evidence and the inferences the tribunal will draw from her/his failure to do so are likely to be adverse.

Explain clearly why you do or do not advise your client to give evidence, but make it clear that it is entirely a matter for her/him to decide. Ask her/him to endorse your papers with her/his decision and, if it is against your advice, include that in the endorsement and warn her/him that the court will ask her/him whether you have explained the consequences of a failure to give evidence.

Should You Call Other Evidence?

Where a potential witness can give helpful evidence of events at which your client was not present, you will usually wish to call her/him. Where the potential witness's evidence is in the main corroborative of your client's, there will not infrequently be inconsistencies between their accounts. To some extent this is inevitable. Several months later people are bound to remember events differently.

Where, however, there is a discrepancy which is only likely to have arisen because someone is lying, it is unlikely you will want to call the potential witness. In this situation it will sometimes happen that your client will tell you that s/he will "speak to" the witness. Explain matter-of-factly that the only evidence you can elicit from that witness is in line with her/his proof of evidence, and that if s/he comes to you with a different account from the one you have already taken, you will not be able to call her/him at all.

You assume your client's version of events is true. If you do call the potential witness, you will confine your questions to those areas in which her/his evidence does not contradict your client's. Because of the likelihood that the prosecutor will expose the evidential conflict in cross-examination, you will only want to call the witness if you feel the benefit of the helpful evidence makes the risk of damage worth taking.

Where a potential witness's evidence is corroborative of your client's, but does not take the case any further, carefully consider how credible s/he appeared to you. Defendants are often convicted by their own witnesses' evidence. Your client's evidence may sound implausible to the tribunal, but they may feel that, as they are not sure s/he has made it up, there is a doubt, and s/he must have the benefit of that doubt. However, an implausible account from a second witness may have a cumulative effect and remove any doubts in the tribunal's minds, leaving them free to convict.

Also, even if they feel quite sure your client is lying in some parts of her/his evidence, they may think this may be a misguided attempt by an innocent and, perhaps, nervous defendant to "improve" her/his case. They are less likely to attribute this motive to a corroborating witness.

Secondly, it is often easy for the prosecutor to "drive a wedge" between the evidence of the defendant and that of her/his witness. If you consider it is better not to call a witness, explain to the client that experience shows that when two people are asked to remember the same event there are nearly always differences in what they remember, and these differences tend to weaken the defence case. You therefore advise it would probably be better not to call the potential witness, but it is your client's decision. S/he can instruct you either:

(a) to call the witness
(b) not to call the witness, or
(c) that s/he leaves the matter to your discretion.

Nearly all clients will leave the decision to your discretion. Ask your client to endorse your papers with her/his decision and, if it is against your advice, include that in the endorsement.

Explain the Procedure to Your Client

A few minutes before you go into court, explain the procedure to your client. Include these points:
1. S/he will be asked name and address
2. S/he will be asked to confirm (or enter) plea
3. The prosecutor will present her/his evidence. If evidence is given which you were not aware of, your client should pass you a note, (for example: "if he was behind the one-way mirror at the end of the aisle he would not have had an unobstructed view—the aisle was full of people").
4. You will call your client to give evidence.
5. The rest of points 6–12 are the same as for any witness (see pages 25–26).
13. You will then call any other defence witnesses and finally address the court.
14. The magistrates will then withdraw to decide their verdict and you will take your client's instructions on mitigation.

Give her/him paper and pen for messages and ask if s/he has any questions. Stress (i) that s/he should ignore the manner in which questions are asked and concentrate on answering accurately; (ii) that s/he should speak very loudly; (iii) and it will be very helpful if s/he will read through her/his proof of evidence several times before going into court and (if there is only one copy) on her/his way to the witness box will hand it to the usher to give to you.

You are now ready to go into court ...

THE PROSECUTION CASE

The opening
Always be ready to note down points from the opening. In a simple case a wise prosecutor will give only a sparse account of what is alleged, hardly supplementing the summons. But there is always the chance s/he will overstate her/his case and give a hostage to fortune. If so, try to note down her/his exact words.

Example:
"The store detective will say that she saw the defendant looking around

very furtively before slipping a jar of coffee into his own shopping-
bag"

Prosecution evidence-in-chief

Never object to a prosecutor leading a police officer at the beginning of
her/his evidence. Never allow a prosecutor to lead a civilian witness on
a single word of her/his evidence even if not a syllable is in dispute.

Your provisional argument (see pages 28–29) is that certain parts of
the witness's evidence cannot be relied on, for certain reasons. As the
witness gives her/his evidence, note down accurately anything which
supports your argument.

Example:
Public Order Act, 1986, s.5
"We chased the group of youths. I caught the defendant Peter. PC
Marshall caught the defendant Paul. The other youths were too far
ahead for us to catch them."

Make a note (not necessarily word-for-word) of any evidence which
contradicts your argument.

Example:
Public Order Act, 1986, s.5
"I particularly distinguished Peter's voice because of his strong Scottish
accent."

Cross-Examination of Prosecution Witnesses

Be careful to cross-examine, not interrogate. Interrogation aims to extract
an admission by putting pressure on the suspect. Cross-examination aims
to lay an evidential foundation for a submission (such as a closing
speech).

Example (a):
The witness says he saw a blue car. He several times denies the
suggestion it was a green car. The interrogator returns to the point
numerous times from different angles. The umpteenth time the witness
says wearily, "I suppose it may have been green".

Example (b):
The witness says he saw a blue car. Under cross-examination he accepts
it was 200 metres away when he first saw it, and that it was driving
away from him at a high speed. He accepts the sun was in his eyes.
He accepts his attention was distracted. He accepts he did not make a
note of the incident until six weeks later, and then did not attach

importance to it. It is put to him that the car was green, and he is adamant it was blue.

An evidential foundation for a closing speech is laid in two ways. You will submit the defence evidence is credible, and that submission can be most effectively made if you have put every part of your case fairly and squarely to any opposing witness who is in a position to comment on it. (In the Crown Court the judge may prohibit you from calling evidence which contradicts testimony you have not challenged, and a County Court judge will attach less weight to such evidence.)

Secondly, you will submit that parts of the prosecution evidence are not sufficiently reliable to base a conviction on. You can make that submission plausibly only if you have to some extent undermined those parts of the evidence.

The possible reasons why one might feel unable to rely on part of a witness's evidence are infinite, but the following categories of reasons frequently recur.

Restricted Observation

Example:

The PC has given evidence that at 4.15 he saw your client trying the door handle of a car index number A123 BCD, parked in Chestnut Road. The defence is that it was not the defendant he saw.

Your argument is that the court cannot be sure, because the PC had an obstructed view of the youth; he never got close to him; and when your client was later arrested he was wearing clothes different from the youth's.

If you put the question of obstruction directly, you may receive the following answer:

Q.   Was your view of the suspect obstructed in any way?
A.   No; I had a perfect view of him and saw him most distinctly.

All that has been achieved is the witness has been allowed to repeat his evidence-in-chief in more detail and more emphatically. You may receive the answer:

Q.   Was your view of the suspect obstructed in any way?
A.   There were a couple of cars, but that was all.

This is a more satisfactory answer, but its value to you has been minimised. The technique is to deal with each point in "small steps".

Example:

Q1.   Officer, were you on the north or south footway of Chestnut Road?

A.   North, sir.

Q2.   Walking east or west?

A.   East, sir.

Q3.   The car you have mentioned, was it parked on the north or the south side of the road?

A.   South, sir.

Q4.   With its driver's-side or its passenger-side next to the footpath?

A.   Passenger's, sir.

Q5.   What sort of a road is Chestnut Road, officer: residential, shopping street, offices, or what?

A.   Residential street, sir.

Q6.   There were cars parked on both sides were there?

A.   Yes, sir.

Q7.   It's a perfectly straight road, is it?

A.   No, sir; it has a slight curve in the middle.

Q8.   What was the weather like?

A.   Quite cold and rather overcast.

Q9.   You saw a young man tampering with the car?

A.   Yes, sir.

Q10.   And as you approached he ran off?

A.   That's right, sir.

Q11.   At that point how far away from him were you?

A.   Let me see; about thirty metres, I would say.

Q12.   You ran after him?

A.   Yes, sir.

Q13.   You didn't catch him?

A.   No, sir.

Q14.   So he ran faster than you?

A.   Afraid so, sir.

Q15.   So you never got closer to him than thirty metres?

A.   That's right, sir.

Q16.   When you made your notes about the incident, did you describe what the young man was wearing?

A.   Let me see, sir. Yes, I put: 'Dressed casually, jeans and tee-shirt'.

Q17.   It was about two hours later after another officer had arrested him that you saw the defendant, wasn't it?

A.   I did see him then, yes sir.

Q18.   What was he wearing?

A.   I don't remember.

Q19.   Wasn't it a long-sleeved blue shirt and brown cotton trousers?

A.   It may have been, sir.

Questions 1–4 establish that the officer was at least the width of a street away from the suspect, and there was at least one parked car between them. In asking those four questions the cross-examiner has taken no risks: answers to those questions could not possibly damage the defence case.

On the basis of the answers to questions 1–8, the cross-examiner will be able to say in her/his speech: "The officer, as you will remember from his evidence, had only a poor opportunity to observe the suspect. On that overcast day, he was on the footpath on the other side of that residential road with cars parked on both sides..."

Never argue the case with the witness. Confine youself to eliciting material for your speech. When you have the material you need on one point, ask no more questions on that topic, but move on to the next one.

Example:
Q6. There were cars parked on both sides, were there?
A.   Yes, sir.
Q7. It's a perfectly straight road, is it?

In your speech you can make the point, "The officer told us there were cars parked on both sides of the road" (which implies that the officer's view of the suspect was obstructed). If you persist with the line of questioning, it might continue thus:

Q. Making it difficult for you to see the suspect, officer?
A. There weren't so many cars parked, sir. At that point there was nothing between me and the defendant except the car he was tampering with.

Bias

Example:
Actual Bodily Harm
The defence case is that the defendant defended himself against the complainant who had first attacked him.
The complainant's father gives evidence that he was quite close when the attack began, and went to intervene.

The prosecutor will probably have elicited from the father details only of what he saw and did. In cross-examination one could question the witness about what he had been doing a few minutes prior to the incident, asking detailed questions to stir the witness's memory. One could then ask what first made the witness aware there was a fight, and ask the witness how he *felt*.

It may become obvious that the father was immediately distressed at the possibility of his son being hurt and could only see the situation in terms of the threat to his son. His denial that his son was in fact the attacker may then carry little weight.

Never come straight out with the point for which you are gathering evidence ("You are biased towards your son, aren't you?"). Think what the points entails (concern for the son, lack of concern for the other man) and approach the point in stages, not letting the witness see what you are getting at.

Previous inconsistent statements

As the witness gives her/his evidence, note any inconsistencies with the original statement. In cross-examiantion, probe the inconsistent evidence. Ask for more details. Coax the witness into as much detail as possible.

Example:
Q. You say Mr Richards bought a take-away meal?
A. Yes.
Q. You saw the take-away shop he went into?
A. Yes.
Q. What was it? Chinese?... Indian?...
A. Chinese.

Coax the witness as far away from the original statement as s/he is readily willing to go. A witness can sometimes be more easily led in a direction apparently opposite to the desired one.

Example:
Q. It must have been very quick, wasn't it?
A. Not that quick.
Q. Under a minute, though?
A. Longer than that.
Q. How long would you say?
A. Perhaps two or three minutes; maybe more.

Get the witness to commit her/himself to the evidence s/he has given.

Example:
Q. Are you quite sure about that?

If appropriate, get the witness to agree that this is an important part of her/his evidence. Then ask the witness whether s/he has made a statement about this matter before. Use an open-ended, non-leading question (if the witness cannot remember making an earlier statement, it will help you). Ask when the previous statement was made. Ask the witness whether s/he told the police the truth. Ask whether s/he told the police everything relevant s/he could remember. Ask whether s/he signed the statement. Ask whether s/he checked its accuracy before signing.

Then obtain the signed original statement from the prosecutor and ask the witness to look at it. Tell her/him to take her/his time. Ask whether it is her/his statement. Ask whether it is her/his signature. Ask where in the statement is the evidence just given.

As soon as you have obtained an answer or answers which undermine the witness's credibility, stop (or proceed with extreme caution). If you allow the witness too much opportunity s/he may be able to recover her/his position.

If your argument is that the witness has lied (whether in the witness box or in the statement) put it to her/him that s/he is trying to protect another, or get the defendant into trouble, or whatever, and has lied for that purpose.

Alternatively, put it to the witness that s/he has given evidence inconsistent with an earlier statement made nearer the time and that her/his memory of the events is not clear, and her/his evidence is not reliable.

Inherent implausibility
If the court can be made to feel "people just do not behave in that way", they will not feel safe in relying on that part of the evidence.

Example:
The complainant has given evidence that the defendant attacked him.
Q. You're twenty-six?
A. Yes.
Q. How tall are you?
A. One metre eighty-eight.
Q. What do you weigh?
A. About eighty-seven kilos.
Q. You do weight-training?
A. Yes.
Q. How often?
A. Usually twice a week.
Q. And how often do you play football?
A. Most Saturdays.
Q. Did you know the defendant is twenty-two?
A. I knew he was about that.
Q. You accept he is one metre seventy?
A. Yes.
Q. And weighs sixty-three kilos?
A. If you say so.
Q. You say he punched you to the face?

A. Yes he did.

Q. What did he stand on?

The technique is to focus on the parts of the evidence which seem implausible without giving the witness an opportunity to explain away the implausibility. The questions have to be put quite briskly and have to be "closed" (tightly restricting the possible answers) to prevent the witness offering an explanation.

Inconsistency with other evidence

The court will be reluctant to place reliance on evidence which does not "fit in" well with the surrounding evidence. A classic example is that a witness's evidence that she was taking a short-cut home may be completely accepted—until a look at the map reveals the short-cut added half a mile to her walk.

The technique is to pin down the witness on the details of her/his evidence and then confront her/him with the surrounding facts ("Would you look at this map?... Do you still say...?")

Inconsistency between witnesses

The technique of "driving a wedge" is dealt with at page 103.

Imprecision

The technique is to open up as many possibilities to the witness as you can, to demonstrate how uncertain s/he is about what happened.

Untruthful witnesses

If your argument is that the witness is deliberately lying, you will aim to discredit her/his evidence (the techniques are outlined at pages 101–105).

Planning your objectives

If you are not ready to cross-examine immediately the prosecutor sits down, apologise to the bench, tell them there is an unexpected point you have to consider, and stare into a law book while you work out your objectives. The delay will only add to the pressure the witness is under. Unless you are clear about your objectives your cross-examination is likely to be ineffective and assist the prosecution.

The most serviceable stance to adopt towards witnesses in one's first cross-examinations is one of absolute neutrality—neither friendly nor unfriendly, aggressive nor timid.

When the witness is in difficulty, you will experience a strong impulse to rescue her/him. Resist it. Remain neutral. Consider how far you can take this line of questioning and what to move onto next.

As a general rule avoid asking questions for the sake of saying something (it is unlikely the witness will give you a helpful answer, and s/he may give a harmful one). An exception is when you receive an "adverse answer".

Adverse answers

In your early cross-examinations you will frequently receive answers "dead against" you which you had not expected. As soon as you realise you are hearing such an answer, think of a completely irrelevant question on the same subject-matter and ask it in a very matter-of-fact manner.

Example:
Answers to your questions have established that the incident took place late in the evening in a street without street lighting.
Q. So visibility was poor?
A. No; the garage next door was floodlit.
Q. Did you see anyone come from the garage?
A. No, it was nearly midnight.

The adverse answer still weakens your case (that cannot be helped) but the fact that you appear unperturbed and seem to regard the adverse answer as not very important, keeps the damage to a minimum.

Habits to avoid

Try to avoid the habit of feeding back to the witness tracts of her/his evidence-in-chief.

Example:
Q. You told us you were on patrol with PC Robinson?
A. Yes, miss.
Q. On foot?
A. Yes, miss.
Q. And you arrived in the High Street?
A. That's right, miss.
Q. At about half-past nine?
A. Yes, miss.

It achieves nothing except conveying an impression that the prosecution evidence is accepted. Even more to be avoided is the habit of cross-examining the prosecution case clearer. The question "Are you sure?" should be used with caution. As a challenge to evidence it is disastrous.

Example:
Q. Are you sure?
A. I'm absolutely certain.

It can alert a dishonest witness to the fact that part of her/his evidence is disputed and give her/him an opportunity to reconsider her/his position.

Example:
A. I paid the tall man with the beard.
Q. Are you sure?
A. Well, it was eight months ago. I'm not sure it was the man with the beard, but I'm quite sure I paid one of the staff.

The one situation in which it is a useful question is to make the witness commit her/himself to her/his evidence before confronting her/him with a previous inconsistent statement or objective evidence such as a map.

No disputed evidence
If none of a particular witness's evidence is disputed, inform the prosecutor s/he may read that witness's statement section 9. The advantage of this procedure is that you know precisely what the evidence will be and there is no risk of the witness adding further evidence against your client.

If the prosecutor nevertheless does call the witness, when s/he has given her/his evidence, if none of it is disputed, remain seated and say "I have no questions".

It sometimes happens that questions from the magistrates elicit new evidence. If this is neutral or favourable to your case then, unless you are fairly sure you can improve upon it with further questions, ask nothing. If the evidence is adverse, deal with it as you would if it had been given in answer to prosecution questions. You are entitled to cross-examine on the replies to the magistrates and, if they are adverse, will need to do so.

Putting your case
Very seldom is there a realistic chance that when you "put" your case, the witness will accept what you are putting. A witness may well accept a preliminary step (for example, that her/his view was obstructed), but is unlikely to accept the full defence case (for example, that the defendant did not tamper with the car).

Nevertheless your case must be put in full and there are two ways in which it can be done. As you go through each part of the evidence you can put what the defendant will say. Alternatively, you can put the whole of your case at once at the end of your cross-examination.

The advantages of putting it in stages are that each part of your case is put in its logical place in the prosecution evidence, and only one part needs to be put at a time.

The advantages of putting it all at the end are that you postpone the time at which you challenge the witness and thereby perhaps prolong the time in which s/he may be more co-operatively disposed; your case may be more effectively put as a whole; and it is easier to avoid forgetting anything which must be put if the whole case is put at once. You can either put the case in questions or by giving the witness the opportunity to comment on each part.

Example:
Q. You first saw the defendant walking towards you, didn't you?
A. No, I saw him climbing out of the window.
Q. And at that point Constable Beyit was not with you, was he?
A. We were both together when we saw him, as I said.
Q. When you said, "Where did you get the bags?" the defendant said, "Over there" and pointed to the shed, didn't he?
A. No; he said, "In there" and put his head back indicating the room he had just climbed out of.

Or:

Q. I put it to you that when you first saw the defendant he was walking towards you.
A. No, he was climbing out of the window.
Q. And you were alone.
A. No, I was with Constable 914 Beyit.
Q. When you asked, "Where did you get the bags?", he replied, "Over there", pointing to the shed.
A. That's not true, it was as I stated.

There is no need to use the phrase "I put it to you" and it is best not to overwork it. An alternative is "I suggest". You may find the procedure is clearer to the witness if you put your case in the form of questions.

Often you will be unable to put your case with absolute precision. Your client may be sure the conversation s/he had with the police was different from what is recorded in their notebooks, but s/he is highly unlikely to be able to remember with certainty each word that was said.

Although you will often have to make it clear to the witness (and thereby the court) that you cannot be definite in the detail of the case you are putting, it is your absolute duty always to put your client's case with complete conviction. You are never allowed to express an opinion on the evidence, or indicate verbally whether you believe your client or any co-defendant guilty or not guilty. But by every non-verbal means, every look, tone, gesture you must convey absolute faith in every syllable of the case you are asserting.

If a police officer vehemently denies part of your client's case, never argue with her/him, but put the next part with even greater vehemence.

Finishing cross-examination

If you have put your case to the witness in stages, attempt to conclude the cross-examination at a point favourable to your case, for example, at a point when the witness has conceded s/he may have got something wrong, or has changed an element of her/his evidence.

Say to the magistrates, "Would you excuse me one moment?" and check over your notes to make sure you have left nothing out. Then say to the witness: "That's all I ask"; "Thank you; that is all"; "I don't think I need ask you anything more; thank you" or an equivalent formula, and sit down.

If you intend to put all of your case to the witness at the end of cross-examination, and are ready to do so, say to the magistrates: "Would you excuse me one moment?", and check over your notes to ensure you have asked everything you need. Put your case to the witness and immediately after her/his last answer use one of the ending-phrases such as "Thank you; that is all", and sit down. If you subsequently realise that you have missed out a part of your case you should have put, ask for leave for the witness to be recalled (if still in court): it will always be given.

Prosecution re-examination

There is very little re-examination in magistrates' courts. If the prosecutor does re-examine, pay close attention. The rule is that s/he may deal only with matters you dealt with in cross-examination but, of course, s/he is entitled to deal with the suggestions behind your questions.

Example:

Your client is accused of theft. You make one of the prosecution witnesses, Dipper, admit she herself has several convictions for theft. The prosecutor then re-examines with a view to showing that Dipper either could not, or is unlikely to have, committed this particular theft.

You cannot object to this. You were attempting to open up the possibility that Dipper might be guilty of this theft, to undermine the case against your client. The prosecutor is therefore entitled to elicit evidence which suggests otherwise. The two categories of evidence which may not be elicited in re-examination are:

    (a) evidence on any matter dealt with in examination-in-chief which was not subject to cross-examination and

    (b) any completely new matter.

It is (obviously) necessary to be quick in objection to re-examination questions. If you are in doubt, rise immediately to your feet and say "Excuse me". Then consider whether the subject-matter really does fall within category (a) or (b) above. If it does, state your objection in a very authoritative voice, but in non-authoritarian terms, such as, "I'm not sure that that arises from cross-examination".

OBJECTING TO PROSECUTION EVIDENCE

Evidence may be objected to under PACE on three grounds: that it was obtained by oppression, or in consequence of something said or done likely to render it unreliable (section 76); or that its admission would be unfair (section 78). Be alert to:

—the point when the PC had grounds for suspecting the defendant of an offence
—the point when the PC had grounds to arrest the defendant
—when the defendant was cautioned
—whether there was any suggestion that anyone else might be arrested
—the evidence identifying the defendant as the offender (was the identification process fair?)

If your client indicates that the police put pressure on her/him (for example, by threatening to arrest a partner, or suggesting the matter would be resolved quickly if the defendant answered questions), your objection will be under sections 76 and 78, which give you more latitude than under section 78 only.

In the Crown Court the general rule is that the judge rules on the admissibility of evidence at the point at which it would be given. In the magistrates' court rulings on admissibility may be sought and given at the following points (among others) in the trial:

(1) As a preliminary point. If the exclusion of the evidence (for example, a confession) would leave no prosecution case, it may be convenient to all parties to determine its admissibility first.

(2) The point in the prosecution case when the evidence occurs. Dealing with the issue of admissibility at this point leaves intact the order of the evidence.

(3) At the close of the prosecution case. This will often be the most satisfactory point at which to raise issues of admissibility.

Before they have heard all the prosecution evidence, magistrates do not feel confident that they know what, taking the case as a whole, it will be fair to admit or exclude, and so lean towards admitting evidence.

At half-time the prosecution case has been fully presented without the defendant having been exposed to the risks of cross-examination.

(4) At the close of the defence case.

The general rule is that the magistrates' court has a wide discretion to conduct a trial as it wishes; therefore although you may make representations as to the point at which you wish the court to rule on the admissibility of evidence, the decision is the court's. The exception to this is that if confession evidence is objected to, the court is obliged to hold a *voire dire*.

The advantage of challenging a confession under section 76 as well as section 78 is that once such a challenge is made it is for the prosecution to prove that the confession was not obtained by the prohibited means at the standard "beyond reasonable doubt".

Under section 78 the prosecution has to show only that the admission of the evidence would not have "such an adverse effect on the fairness of the proceedings that the court ought not to admit it". The standard of proof at which this must be shown is not stated. However, the words "such an effect" and "the court may refuse to allow evidence" indicate that the evidential burden placed on the prosecution by section 78 is lighter than that placed by section 76.

There is no advantage in challenging admission solely under section 76; section 78 can always be added as an alternative.

It is often possible to lay an adequate foundation for your objection without antagonising the police witnesses. For example, it may be undisputed that the police arranged for a confrontation between the Victim and the defendant: your point may be that, in the circumstances, fairness required an identification parade. As long as your client's version of what happened is fully "put", an adequate foundation has been laid for the objection.

In other cases there will be a dispute on the evidence. For example, your point may be that at an early stage the officer had ample grounds to arrest the defendant and therefore should not have continued questioning her/him on the street. In such a case you must put to the officer that at a specified point s/he had grounds for arrest. You must list the grounds so the officer can say why s/he disagrees with you.

It is not, however, necessary to put to the officer that if s/he should have arrested the defendant, it follows s/he should not have continued questioning her/him. This is because, firstly, it is a hypothetical question (as the officer does not accept s/he should have made the arrest when you claim s/he should); and secondly the question is a matter for the bench to decide.

Making your submission
Depending upon the point in the proceedings at which you make your submission, it may come as a surprise to the magistrates that there is any objection to the evidence.

It is usually unwise to seek a ruling on admissibility as a preliminary point unless the prosecutor is in favour of this course, as your request is likely to be refused and you may start off, to some extent, on the wrong foot with the magistrates. If your application is made at the end of either the prosecution or the defence case, it will probably assist the court if you explain why you are making it at this stage.

Example:

"May it please you, sir; before opening the defence case I seek a ruling on a matter of law.

"In my submission a certain passage in PC Plumley's evidence, which is repeated in PC Shaddhoe's evidence, should be excluded.

"I raise the matter at this point because, as you and your colleagues, sir, are judges of both fact and law it seems unnecessary and undesirable to interrupt the flow of the evidence for a ruling and, as my point is that it is unfair to admit that evidence, the court can better assess that now it has heard the entire prosecution case."

As with all submissions begin by stating the ruling you seek.

Example:

"I ask you, sir, to exclude the passage in PC Helmholtz's evidence, and the corresponding passage in PC Corcoran's evidence, beginning, 'I said to him "Where have you just come from?..."' down to '"I met Sidney outside the kebab shop".'"

State whether you are seeking exclusion under section 78 or both sections.

A Working Plan for a section 78 Objection

(1) *Explain why you are making the objection at this point*

(2) *State the ruling you seek*

(3) *Outline the legal basis of the objection, e.g. from Walsh (1989) Cr App R 161, and/or from the relevant Code*

(4) *Contrast the course of events envisaged by the Code with what actually happened*

(5a) *Submit that although no-one is at fault, the evidence falls below the necessary high standard*

or:

(5b) *Submit that the flagrant disregard of the Code makes the breach significant and substantial*

    Alladice (1988) 87 Cr. App. R. 380 and Walsh are cases in point

Objecting to Evidence Under section 78

If your objection is based on breaches of the codes of practice, outline in a sentence why the breaches should lead to exclusion.

Example:

"My submission will be that the breaches taken together are significant and so substantial as to have such an adverse effect on the fairness of the trial that the evidence should be excluded."

Begin by citing authority in support of the proposition that generally unfairness will result from significant and substantial breaches of the codes (*Walsh* (1989) 91 Cr App R 161 is a case in point).

It is generally wise to avoid any suggestion of criticism of the police but to indicate what the codes state should happen and why the particular provision (caution, legal advice, or whatever) is an important safeguard of the fairness of the procedure. Contrast this with what actually happened, demonstrating that the breach or breaches are significant and substantial.

Stress that it is not a question of whether or not the particular passage of evidence is accurate but of whether it is fair to rely on evidence obtained in a way different from what parliament intended. You can finish in this way:

Example:

"You may wish to approach making your ruling in this way, ma'am; by considering, firstly, whether there were breaches of the codes; if you find there were not, you will, of course, admit the evidence; if you find there were breaches, then it may be that you will be slow to find it acceptable to admit such evidence."

Although it is repeatedly stated (*e.g. Canale* [1990] 2 All E.R. 187) that it is no part of the function of admissibility rulings to discipline the police, nevertheless a flagrant disregard of the codes by the police is a factor which may "make substantial or significant [breaches] which might not otherwise be so" (*Walsh* (1989) 91 Cr. App. R. 161). It will be worth drawing the court's attention to this line of authority in any "flagrant breach" case.

Your objection may not be based on breaches of the codes but some other sort of unfairness. For example, three weeks after he was robbed the complainant may see (and cause to be arrested) the defendant, whom he identifies as the robber. In this sort of case, it may well be that the defendant will not give evidence (all s/he can say is that s/he had never seen the complainant before). You can therefore make a closing speech attacking the adequacy of the identification evidence. Alternatively, you can apply for that evidence to be excluded under section 78 (at any of the four points in the trial referred to above).

An advantage of taking such a point at the close of the prosecution case is that you may be going to call alibi evidence. It may well be that after hearing the (perhaps unconvincing) alibi evidence and the evidence of the defendant, the magistrates will be sure of the defendant's guilt; whereas at half-time they may have been willing to exclude the identification evidence. A section 78 submission in such a case would be based on *Turnbull* [1977] Q.B. 224 and identical to one made as a closing speech (except for the standard of proof).

A Working Plan for a *Voire Dire*

(1) *Confine your cross-examination of the police witnesses to the inducements, threats or oppression; putting to them the defendant's version of what happened*

(2) *Confine the defendant's evidence to the same issue and ensure the prosecutor does not ask the defendant whether the confession is true*

(3) *In submission, emphasize the irrelevance to this ruling of whether or not the confession is true; and the high standard of proof at which the prosecution have to prove the confession was not obtained by the prohibited means*

Objecting to Evidence Under section 76

If your client instructs you that s/he made a confession (that is, any statement wholly or partly adverse to her/him) because of any sort of inducement or threat, you have a tactical choice of objecting to the admission of the confession under section 78 alone (admission would be unacceptably unfair) or under sections 76 and 78. The advantages of relying on section 78 alone are:

(a) objection to the evidence can be taken at any stage of the trial (subject to the discretion of the court to regulate its own procedure. In practice, you will be allowed to make your objection at the close of the prosecution or defence case if you so wish).

(b) your objection may be more likely to succeed under section 78. A section 76 objection may force the court into deciding for or against the police, whereas a section 78 objection can be couched in terms which are not critical of anyone.

The advantages of relying on sections 76 *and* 78 are:

(a) the prosecution have to prove beyond reasonable doubt that the confession was properly obtained.

(b) you are entitled as of right to have the admissibility of the confession determined at a *voire dire* hearing which allows the defendant to give evidence and undergo cross-examination restricted to the circumstances of the confession.

If there is to be a *voire dire*, inform the prosecutor before the trial begins, so that in her/his opening s/he will refer to the confession as a matter on which the court has to rule, rather than as an established part of the prosecution's evidence. If there is an opportunity it may be wise to inform the clerk that there will be a *voire dire*.

The prosecutor will then call the evidence in the usual way up to the point at which the first of the police officers finishes that part of her/his evidence dealing with the confession. You will then cross-examine her/him only in relation to the confession (of course it may be necessary to deal with events which happened much before the confession if they are relevant to the inducements, threats or oppression), putting to her/him the defendant's version of what happened. The rest of the police witnesses will then give their evidence in relation to the confession, upon which you will cross-examine them.

It is very likely that you will call the defendant. You should restrict her/his evidence to why s/he came to make the confession, including, of course, any background evidence needed to make the explanation intelligible.

Cross-examination should be restricted to whether the confession was properly obtained. If the prosecutor asks the defendant whether it is true, you should object (*Wong Kam-ming v. R.* [1979] 2 W.L.R. 81; *Davis* [1990] Crim L.R. 860). After re-examination of your last witness, use a formula such as "May it please you, ma'am; that is the defence evidence on the *voire dire*".

The prosecutor will then make a submission that the evidence was properly obtained and should be admitted; you then submit that whether or not the magistrates consider it more likely than not that the evidence was properly obtained, it has not been proved beyond reasonable doubt. On that strict test the prosecution fail and the evidence must be excluded.

If the evidence is excluded no further reference may be made to anything said on the *voire dire* by defence witnesses (including the defendant). Thus it cannot be put to a defence witness that on the *voire dire* s/he made a statement inconsistent with her/his evidence in the trial proper.

If the evidence is ruled admissible anything said by defence witnesses (including the defendant) on the *voire dire* is treated as any other statement, and can be put to the witness as a previous inconsistent statement and, if s/he denies making it, proved (under the Criminal Procedure Act 1865, s.4).

A previous inconsistent statement of a prosecution witness made on the *voire dire* can always be put to her/him and, if s/he denies making it, proved.

Close of the Prosecution Case

At this point, consider two matters. Have the prosecution called some evidence on each element of each charge? If there are two or more charges it is easy to overlook a lack of (often formal) evidence on a minor charge. Examples of points to check are: lack of consent to motor vehicle interference; evidence of identification of vehicle or premises; and that an officer was acting in the execution of her/his duty.

If there is such a gap in the prosecution case, deal with it as follows.

Example:
"Ma'am; dealing only with the second charge, that of motor vehicle interference, I submit that there is no case to answer.

"As you are well aware, the onus is on the prosecution to satisfy you so you are sure of each element of each charge. If the evidence is less than that, the prosecution must fail. If there is no evidence at all on any one element, then there is no case to answer.

"The prosecution cannot ask the court to make presumptions, and certainly the court will not draw inferences which the prosecution have not expressly asked it to.

"To prove motor vehicle interference, it is not enough to prove a person touched a vehicle, or even got into it. He may have been perfectly entitled to. It is for the prosecution to prove he was not.

"Ma'am, [the victim's] statement says he owns vehicle A123 BCD and left it parked in Ratchett Avenue. You will have heard many similar statements, I'm afraid, and will be aware that they continue: 'I gave nobody permission to touch the vehicle'. This statement does not.

"Because there is no evidence of lack of permission, I submit, ma'am, that on the charge of motor vehicle interference there is no case to answer."

It is, of course, also possible to make a submission on the basis that some of the evidence was so unclear or was so undermined in cross-examination that it cannot be convicted on.

This is rare in simple summary cases largely because the evidence is that of professional witnesses. However, if you think there is any chance, make a submission. If the magistrates feel that on the evidence they have heard alone they could not convict, they may throw a minor charge out at this stage to concentrate on the real issues. Remember that the prosecution case is at its weakest at the end of the prosecution evidence.

The second matter is whether, now you have heard all the prosecution evidence, you need to speak to your client. If so, ask for five minutes to take instructions. If you had not been provided with prosecution witness statements, you can mention (without complaining) that this is the first time you have heard the prosecution evidence.

Do not, at this stage, suggest changing her/his plea to your client. If s/he does change, s/he is likely to resent the pressure such a suggestion creates at such a moment. If s/he does not, her/his confidence in her/his case and/or you, will diminish.

If s/he makes the suggestion, then unless it is obviously born of the pressure of the moment, treat it seriously as you do any (realistic) suggestion of any client. Ask the court for more time. Unless your client is quite sure s/he wants to change plea (and has endorsed your instructions) continue with the trial. There is no special form of endorsement for any change of instructions, but if it is against your advice, make sure that is included.

THE DEFENCE CASE

The Defendant's Evidence-in-Chief

Retrieve her/his proof of evidence from your client and begin as follows.

> *Example:*
> "May it please you, ma'am, I call the defendant."
> (The usher swears the defendant)
> "Please give the court your full name."
> "What is your address?"

Nearly always witnesses speak much too quietly. In a very warm friendly way make it clear to the defendant that s/he must be audible. It is as well to do this at the beginning because an inaudible witness will cause genuine problems to the magistrates, and it will be easier for the witness to get used to speaking loudly at the start. Encourage her/him to face the bench.

If your client is of good character, establish that at the beginning. If s/he has only one or two old convictions, especially if they are unrelated, it may be preferable to admit them rather than allow the magistrates to assume s/he probably has many previous convictions. If your client does wish to admit such convictions (and s/he must decide and endorse your instructions) put them in at the beginning.

If s/he is of good character, then put in one or two indicators of conventional social respectability (marriage; church; home-ownership; philanthropic activities; academic achievement). If the magistrate interrupts with: "What is the relevance of this, Ms Snooks?" you have been presented with an early opportunity to address the bench directly. Make the most of it. Tell the court that credibility and character are in issue, and you want the court to know what sort of wo/man your client is. Always understate your case (before the evidence has been given).

If your client is not of good character you may be able to get in an indicator or two of conventional respectability without putting character in issue, for instance, long marriage; long period with the same employer; home-ownership.

Getting started

Defence examination-in-chief in a short case is not difficult. Your client has read her/his proof of evidence. Her/his version of events will be relatively straightforward and you have discussed any difficulties in it with her/him. You can usually get started very easily.

Example:
"You have just heard the evidence of the police officer who told us that on Tuesday 14th June this year at about half-past two in the afternoon you were in Acacia Road. Why were you there?"

"Not leading" is not really a problem. Once you have got your client started, a few prodding questions should steer her/him through her/his account.

It is usually best to deal with each witness's evidence in chronological order and occasionally you may have to begin with evidence which precedes the prosecution evidence.

Example:
Your client is charged with shoplifting.
The principal evidence against him is closed circuit TV film. He was interviewed only briefly by the police when he admitted taking the goods without paying for them but said he did not realise what he was doing.
In conference he has explained to you that about a week earlier he had begun taking prescribed medication which put him into a dazed state in which he "didn't know what he was doing".

An easy way to get him started is:

Q. How well do you remember the events of Tuesday 5th March?
A. I remember being arrested and taken to the police station, but my memory of what happened before that is very hazy.
Q. Why is that?
A. I wasn't feeling very well.
Q. When had you begun feeling unwell?
A. About two weeks before, I ... etc...

But it may be that you would prefer to establish the medical difficulties before dealing with the events of 5th March. You can get your client started in this way:

Q. What is your address?
A. 26 Laburnam Grove, Midchester.
Q. Are you working?
A. I have a job, but I've been on sick leave for the last two months.
Q. When did you first have to see your doctor?
A. In the last week of February, I ...

Or in this way:

Q. Have you needed to see your doctor at any time this year?
A. Several times.
Q. Why did you have to see her the first time this year?
A. Towards the end of February, I ...

As far as possible always let your client tell her/his own story in the way that is most natural to her/him. Unless the order in which s/he originally told it to you was difficult to follow, let her/him give her/his evidence in that order. Devise an opening question which will elicit a reference to the starting-point of your client's story, and let her/him go on from there.

As your client is giving her/his evidence you should act as the mouthpiece of the court. As s/he gets into the flow of the story, tell her/him that notes are being taken and s/he should watch the pens. Your client may adapt the pace of her/his evidence. If s/he does not, say, "Pause" from time to time, followed by "Yes?" to break the narrative up into passages which can be taken down.

If s/he says anything which the magistrates are unlikely to understand, ask questions to make your client's evidence clear. As soon as s/he has finished her/his evidence, say, "Would you remain there, please", and sit down.

It is unlikely in the extreme that your client will change her/his plea when actually giving evidence in chief but if s/he should do so, remember that you cannot take instructions until s/he has finished giving evidence.

First, make absolutely sure s/he understands what s/he is being asked. Secondly, consider to which of the charges your client's evidence amounts to a plea of Guilty. Ask her/him: "So you accept you are guilty of...[that charge]?" When s/he says Yes, ask: "And so when you have finished giving evidence you would wish that charge to be put again so you can change your plea?"

Then continue with the rest of her/his evidence. If s/he admits all the charges, say to the court: "Sir, I have no further questions. In the light of the admissions the defendant has made I wonder if the court would be minded to allow the charges to be put again?"

Cross-examination of the defendant

Generally you will not want to have to object to any questions put to your client in cross-examination, but you may have to object if the prosecutor invites her/him to speculate; or if a factual matter is misrepresented to your client. If the questioning is irrelevant or repetitious it is usually better to give your opponent the fullest opportunity to exasperate the magistrates.

Re-examination

Very little re-examination takes place in magistrates' courts, but it can be a vital opportunity to uphold your case.

Your opponent has challenged your client's evidence by suggesting it is implausible ("people do not behave like that"); self-contradictory; or inconsistent with the objective evidence. In re-examination your aim is to show that any inconsistencies or implausibilities are apparent rather than real. The principal way this is done is by putting the evidence in context.

Example:

Pros. Damage was done to the shop on three occasions?

A. That's what you say.

Pros. You admit that on each occasion you were present on the opposite side of the road?

A. I didn't see anyone doing any damage.

Pros. But you were in Clitheroe Street on Monday 5th at 7.40 p.m.; Thursday 8th at 8.55 p.m.; and Wednesday 14th at 8.25 p.m.?

A. I said I was there.

Pros. It's just coincidence, is it?

A. I don't know.

Pros. Thank you; no further questions.

Def. On the opposite side of the road to the antique shop, are there any shops?

A. Yes.

Def. What shops?

A. The chip shop; there's a newsagent's; I think there's a...

Def. Let me stop you there. Do you go into any of those shops?

A. The chip shop; sometimes the newsagent's, maybe...

Def. How often do you go into the chip shop?

A.   Most nights.
Def.   At about what time?
A.   No set time. It depends.
Def.   What does it depend on?
A.   Who's about, what's happening, when we feel hungry.
Def.   Who's "we"?
A.   My mates.
Def.   Do you usually go to the chip shop with your mates?
A.   That's where we hang out, in front of the chip shop.
Def.   What do you mean by "hang out"?
A.   There's always people there. It's where we meet.
Def.   How many evenings in an ordinary week would you be outside the chip shop?
A.   It depends. Most evenings. Not Fridays. Friday we go to the youth club.

You should be very business-like in re-examination, and you will be if you are clear about what you are trying to achieve. If, at any point, your opponent should interrupt: "I'm not sure that this point arises out of cross-examination", you should be able immediately to reply.

Example:
"The suggestion underlying my friend's questioning seemed to be that there was something suspicious about the defendant's banking arrangements. The purpose of my questioning is to rebut that suggestion by eliciting evidence that his banking arrangements had been long in place, and there had been good reasons for them. If my friend accepts there is nothing suspicious about the arrangments then I have no further questions on the subject."

Remember that you are not allowed to lead in re-examination. Forced-choice questions are often useful.

Example:
Q.   Did you remain there?
A.   No.
Q.   Did you return home or go somewhere else?
A.   I went home.

The end of the defendant's evidence
When you have finished your re-examination ask the magistrate, "I don't know whether you, sir, have any questions for the defendant?"

If your client's replies to the questions from the magistrate leave your case in a less favourable light, you should re-examine.

Often in re-examination you will meet suggestions from the prosecution head-on; for example, the prosecution suggestions that the banking arrangements were suspicious being countered with evidence showing they were perfectly ordinary. Suggestions which emanate from the court you should usually avoid meeting head-on. You may ask the same questions and receive the same answers but your manner should be less combative, more persuasive.

At the end of your client's evidence, say to her/him, "Thank you, Ms X, please would you return to the dock." Do not ask the court to "release" the defendant: s/he has to remain to the end of the case.

Defence witnesses

If the witness has no previous convictions, begin by asking questions to elicit her/his good character and social respectability. If there are previous convictions, it may be possible to slip in one or two signs of respectability under the guise of questions to put the witness at her/his ease, but take care: witnesses do not have shields to lose.

If the witness was present at the alleged offence it is highly unlikely that the prosecutor will object to your leading on time and place, but always ask, and always acknowledge to the court that you are leading.

Example:

Q. I'm leading with permission, ma'am: Mr Griggs, on Tuesday 6th May this year at about 7.15 in the evening, you were in Dulchester High Street, weren't you?
A. Yes.
Q. Why were you there?...

In the rare case when the prosecutor objects to your leading to get the witness started, begin in this way:

Q. Mr Potts, you have come to court today to give evidence about something you witnessed, haven't you?
A. Yes.
Q. Was it something which happened indoors or out of doors?
A. Out of doors.
Q. Where?
A. The High Street.
Q. Which High Street?
A. Dulchester High Street.
Q. Are you able to remember the date it happened?
A. No; it was about two months ago.
Q. At what time of day did you arrive in the High Street?
A. About early evening.
Q. What were you doing in the High Street at that time?...

CLOSING SPEECH

Preparation

Many newly-qualified advocates are anxious about having to make a closing speech, often because they feel they may be able to find little to say. That is not necessarily a disadvantage. The general rule is always to make your points in as few words as possible. After a short case, a long speech tends to suggest one needs to argue hard to have any hope of justifying an acquittal.

Very briefly run down your elements/evidence table so that you have at your fingertips exactly what the prosecution had to prove.

Your Argument

Think of the defence closing speech as a reply to the prosecution opening speech.

The prosecution opening indicated both what it hoped to prove and how it intended to prove it. The purpose of your speech is to show either that the prosecution has failed to discharge its burden of proof; or that you have succeeded in discharging a burden of proof on you (for example, reasonable excuse). Each line of argument should be illustrated by

Example:

Argument:	Evidence:
Def.'s overall account of his visit to supermarket corroborated by store detective	she accepted he had stopped and hesitated by the toothpaste and the biscuits as he said
Def. could not have known what store detective would say on this	Evidence about this was not included in the store detective's witness statement
Def. likely to be right that his manner was not "furtive"	Evidence shows there were numerous staff and security personnel, none of whom noticed anything suspicious
Detective's impression coloured by Def.'s act	This was first time she had noticed Def.
Def.'s change of attitude consistent with mistake	When Def. first stopped he was very indignant; when unpaid-for goods produced, he was apologetic

reference to the evidence (both the favourable and unfavourable parts). It is usually prudent to include all the points which occur to you. You may begin with a strong one and save another strong point for last; alternatively you may deal with the points chronologically as they arose in the evidence.

Deal with the evidence as lightly as you can. Quote it as little as possible. As far as you can, do not comment on the manner in which it was given. If you feel one of your witnesses gave her/his evidence badly, comment very lightly.

Example:
(The witness was very confused)
"Making an honest attempt to remember as well as he could."

Try to avoid dotting the i's and crossing the t's.

Example:
"You heard evidence that the defendant was stopped near the place the offence was committed. There was also evidence that several other people of about his age and description were present at the same place."

Leave it at that. If the thought "Why should it have been the defendant who committed the offence, rather than any of the others?" arises in the minds of the court it is more effective than if you suggest it to them.

Almost certainly there is at least one reason why it is more likely to have been the defendant: go straight on to deal with that evidence.

Example:
"In fact the only thing the prosecution can rely on to suggest that of the twenty of so young people there, it was the defendant who had committed this offence, is that a screwdriver was found on him.

"I would make three points. Firstly, none of the other youths was searched. The court will not wish to speculate about whether or not any of the others had on him a screwdriver or something else with which the marks could have been made.

"Secondly, I hope it is accepted by the court that the defendant had a perfectly good reason for having that tool with him.

"Thirdly, there is nothing to show any screwdriver was used in committing this offence, still less this particular screwdriver. That is a speculation of the prosecution."

Stock Components

Three of the points you may want to make, occur so frequently that you should have ready-made submissions to be slotted into your speeches as appropriate. They are: identification; a missing element; and a gap in continuity.

Identification

As soon as you discover identification will be in issue, ask the court for its copies of *R v. Turnbull* [1977] Q.B. 224 and *Reid v. The Queen* [1990] 1 A.C. 363. Adapt your stock submission to the particular facts.

Example:
"This was clearly a very nasty incident—sure everyone in the court has sympathy with the Victim—because of nastiness of incident court will, of course, consider the identification evidence very carefully—especially in view of the fact that defendant man of good character—respectfully remind court of "special need for caution" —court will want to "examine closely" circumstances of the identification—length of observation was ......—at distance of ......—witness had ... opportunities of seeing the suspect before—in *Turnbull* court considered quality of identification evidence good when identification was after long period of observation, or by a relative, neighbour, close friend, etc—evidence considered poor when it is fleeting glance or longer observation made in difficult conditions—when quality is poor a case is withdrawn from the jury—I submit that evidence in this case, because of relatively brief opportunity Victim had of seeing offender, is more towards "poor" end of scale—also draw court's attention to case of *Reid*—"a mere statement that a jury must treat visual identification with extreme caution ... was not sufficient"—"difficult to convey ... the reality of particular dangers which exist in the evidence without drawing to the attention of the jury two things which they are unlikely to know ... experience in the courts over the years has shown that in a not insignificant number of cases erroneous identification evidence by apparently honest witnesses has led to wrong convictions"—here, of course, the witnesses are obviously honest people— "second thing which the jury are unlikely to know is the substantial degree of risk that honest witnesses may be wrong in their evidence of identification ... essential to distinguish between honesty and accuracy and not to assume the latter because of belief in the former ... honesty as such is no guarantee against a false impression being so indelibly

imprinted on the mind as to convince an honest witness that it was wholly reliable."

Missing Element

One reason for preparing a table of elements/evidence in a case, is to see at a glance whether the prosecution have adduced evidence on every element. In the magistrates' court it not infrequently happens that a small but necessary part of the evidence is missing.

If there is more than one charge, then, unless the missing part is common to all the charges (for example, identification evidence), you will have made a submission of No Case in relation to that charge only (see page 51).

Where your client faces only one charge it is generally safer to call no defence evidence, and proceed to your closing speech. If you make a half-time submission, it is possible the magistrates will allow the prosecution to reopen its case to put in the missing evidence.

A speech seeking an acquittal on the basis of a missing element of the offence is necessarily going to be short and, as it does not deal with the merits of the case, may well be unattractive.

The attitude you should convey to the court is that as the prosecution, for whatever reason, has not provided evidence of one element, the court will be bound, sooner or later, to acquit and you are helping it to do so with the least waste of everyone's time and without appearing to be point-scoring against the prosecutor.

Example:
"May it please you, ma'am; I call no evidence and close the defence case and proceed to address you in closing—Although there are a number of points I could make about the prosecution case, there is one aspect of it which I have to submit makes it incapable of founding a safe conviction—that being so, it seems right to save the court's time by restricting myself to what is effectively one submission—the court will remember the evidence of Mrs Potter—her evidence would strike a lay person as rather odd because she explains that her house was broken into and then makes the rather fatuous point that 'she gave no-one permission to do that—of course the reason such a statement has to be made is that part of the definition of burglary is that it is entry as a trespasser—the prosecution must prove as part of its case that the entry was without permission—my submission is, of course, that the prosecution has not proved that and therefore has not made out its case—the court will remember the evidence of Mr Parker— that he saw the defendant leaving 43, Acacia Drive—there is no

evidence even to suggest either that the defendant had no permission to visit No. 43, or that there ever was a burglary at No. 43—Mrs Potter's statement merely refers to "my address, which is known to the police"—it could be anywhere—the fact that a statement by the householder stating that he or she gave no-one permission to break in is necessary is shown by the fact that such a statement forms part of the prosecution evidence in every burglary case—it is necessary proof of an element of the offence—here, there is no evidence that there has ever been a burglary at the address alleged in the charge—it therefore follows in my submission that the prosecution case is not made out."

Lack of Continuity

Inadequate identification evidence is one species of continuity problem.

Example:
It is not disputed that a person drove car index number A123 BCD without insurance. What evidence is there to link this person with the defendant in the dock?

In identification cases there is nearly always prima facie evidence: the issue is whether the witness's identification of the defendant as the offender is reliable at the criminal standard of proof.

The other category of continuity problem usually concerns fingerprints or drugs, and generally a link in the chain is missing completely.

Example:
Scenes of crime officer: "On 1st June, I lifted from a knife labelled 'Exhibit JD1', a set of fingerprints which I labelled 'SC1' and sent to the police laboratory".
Fingerprint expert: "On 7th June at the police laboratory I compared a set of fingerprints labelled 'SC1' with a set of fingerprints in the name of Leonard Blenkinsop and I have no doubt they were made by the same person."

"May it please you, sir; I call no evidence and I close the defence case and proceed to address you in closing. There are a number of points I could make about the evidence which has been called for the prosecution, but as there is one point which, I submit, makes it impossible for a safe conviction to be based upon it, it may best assist the court for me to deal solely with it.

"This is, of course, a very serious and unpleasant allegation, and therefore the court is especially concerned to examine the evidence with care.

"The prosecution has brought this case against this defendant and it is for them to show the court—step by step—how the evidence they have collected leads inevitably to a finding of the accused's guilt.

"If the prosecution leave out any one step in that process and ask the court—in effect—to make any assumptions against the defendant, then the prosecution are seeking to reduce the court to a mere rubber-stamp for a finding of guilt already made by the police.

"The prosecution have called some circumstantial evidence, and it may well be that the court thinks that on its own it amounts to very little.

"The only hard evidence in the case is fingerprint evidence, and that being so, it is obviously of especial importance that that evidence indisputably implicates the defendant.

"What that means in practice, I submit, is three things. Firstly, that fingerprints are found in circumstances such that they must be those of the offender. Secondly, that a set of fingerprints is taken which certainly belongs to the accused. And thirdly, there is conclusive expert evidence that the two sets were made by the same person. And all this must be shown at the high, criminal, standard of proof.

"Quite clearly, in my submission, the prosecution have failed to prove their case. They have not called any evidence whatsoever to establish that fingerprints were ever taken from this defendant.

"The fingerprints which the officer said he compared with those found on the knife were, and I quote from the officer's evidence-in-chief, "a set of fingerprints in the name of Leonard Blenkinsop". Those words are not, of course, evidence that the fingerprints were the defendant Mr Blenkinsop's. Anything written on the fingerprint form is clearly hearsay. There was no evidence as to whose those fingerprints were, and certainly no evidence to connect either set of fingerprints to the defendant.

"Sir, it is for the prosecution to prove each step of the case against the defendant. In my submission, they have produced no evidence whatsoever which implicates him in this offence and I therefore, on his behalf, ask you to find this case not proved."

(The hearsay point is dealt with on page 9).

A Working Plan for a Defence Closing Speech

(1)   *Outline your argument*

(2)   *State the matters of fact and law which fall to be decided by the tribunal*

(3)   *Set out the standard of proof, and (if it is good) the defendant's character*

(4a)   *Argue point by point how the evidence falls short of proving the defendant's guilt* or

(4b) *Argue that the evidence proves your client's defence*
(5)   *Summarise the points you have made*

Making your speech

Your speech should always have an argument. The prosecutor opened her/his case by outlining how the evidence would prove your client's guilt. Your speech outlines the ways in which the evidence falls short of doing so. Always begin by saying what you are going to say.

Example:
"May it please you, sir; you have heard two significantly different accounts of what took place on the afternoon of 19th March. My principal submission is, of course, that Mr Jones' account is not so obviously more credible than the defendant's that you could be satisfied you are sure events happened as he described.

"If you are with me on that, sir, that would, obviously, be decisive of the case. But in case you are against me on that point, my secondary submission is that even if the facts were as Mr Jones has them, as a matter of law the offence would not be made out as there is no evidence of a threat of immediate personal violence."

Outline the matters which the court has to decide: that is, which elements of the alleged offences are in issue and which are undisputed; and any defence upon which your client relies.

It is always prudent to state the burden and standard of proof and, in any case where it is the prosecution who bear the burden of *dis*proving a defence (self-defence, for example) it is vital. It must be done tactfully, as magistrates generally feel themselves to be conversant with these matters. Phrases such as "as you are well aware" can be useful. One approach is to intertwine dealing with the standard of proof with dealing with the evidence.

Example:
"It may well be that you and your colleagues feel some doubt about the speed of the BMW, and if you are not satisfied you are sure you will of course leave that point entirely out of your consideration of how long the witness had the defendant in her sight."

If your client's character is good, point out that that *as a matter of law* goes both to her/his credibility, and to the likelihood of her/his committing an offence. Then argue point by point how the evidence falls short of proving at least one element of the prosecution case. Illustrate your argument with reference to the evidence, but quote it only when you need to comment on the actual words used. End by summarising what you have said. Do not allow yourself to re-argue any of the points you have already made, but in outline form indicate how your line of argument leads to the defendant's acquittal.

Stipendiary magistrate

It is generally prudent when addressing a lay bench, to deal with any matters of law fully and even emphatically.

When addressing a stipendiary, deal with the law very lightly, making the assumption s/he is entirely familiar with the burden and standard of proof; the elements of the offence(s), and any relevant case-law. With this exception, you should make exactly the same speech to a stipendiary that you would to a lay bench. If you feel your speech needs to be shortened for the stipendiary, ask yourself why. If you feel it is unnecessary to make some of the points to a stipendiary, then it would almost certainly be unnecessary to make them to a lay bench.

The other difference with a stipendiary is that s/he will usually give her/his verdict immediately upon the close of your speech. If it is an acquittal, ask for your client's costs from Central Funds (unless s/he is legally aided with a nil contribution).

If it is a conviction and you had insufficient time to prepare mitigation earlier, then unless a pre-sentence report is clearly necessary, ask the magistrate to put the case back in the list for ten minutes for you to take instructions. Most stipendiary magistrates in these circumstances will have effectively decided whether or not they require a report and, if not, will be happy for you to take instructions on the defendant's means.

Preparation for mitigation

When the bench retires to deliberate its verdict, consider whether there are any applications you need to make if your client is acquitted.

The only common application is for costs to be paid from Central Funds and any contribution to a legal aid order to be returned to the defendant. If the defendant is legally aided with a nil contribution, obviously this is unnecessary.

There are more points to consider in preparation for a verdict of Guilty. The circumstances in which you would seek to have your client sentenced without an up-to-date pre-sentence report are dealt with at page 144. If relevant, prepare a speech in mitigation (see pages 144–157). If you think the convicting magistrates may refuse your client bail pending the preparation of the pre-sentence report, prepare a bail application (see pages 135–144). If your client had been in custody prior to the trial, it is unlikely s/he will be given bail pending sentence. However, you may well be able to argue that s/he has done so great a proportion of any likely sentence that it is very unlikely s/he will abscond at this stage, and that the Probation Service will be enabled to prepare a fuller report if they see the defendant in the community.

No matter how strongly you may feel that your client should not have been convicted, it is usually better to defer advising on appeal until you have had an opportunity to reflect on the trial.

CHAPTER 3

CRIMINAL TRIAL—PROSECUTION

PREPARATION

You will generally be prosecuting a "list" of summary trials, which you will have been given only the night before. It is important, therefore, to prepare the cases efficiently: aim to read each page only once. Have three sheets of paper to hand, for "Witnesses", "Opening" and "Notes". First check the file front. Is the case actually set for trial at the time and court you expect? Have all the defendants pleaded Not Guilty? Is it a full trial or Newton trial? Are there any messages for you?

Then check the inside back cover of the file ("page 3"). Is the latest endorsement relevant to you? Then look for recent memoranda and correspondence. Is there a recent letter from defence solicitors notifying a change of plea to Guilty? From the witness warning form, copy the names of those warned onto your "Witnesses" list. Put "section 9" against the names of any witnesses whose statements have been served under that provision. Check that the witnesses have been warned for the correct time of day.

Then untag the central part of the file and find the charge sheet and "brief facts". Read the charge sheet and (unless you are very familiar with the offence in question) look it up in *Blackstone's*, *Archbold*, or *Anthony & Berryman*. On your "Opening" sheet write down in note form the charges and their elements.

Example:
Criminal damage

—defendant destroys/damages
—property belonging to another
—intending to damage/destroy or being reckless as to whether damage/destruction caused

Then read the first witness statement carefully. Was it made sufficiently contemporaneously to be used in the witness box to refresh memory? As a rule of thumb, up to three weeks is probably acceptable (*Fotheringham* [1975] Crim L.R. 710). If the statement does not contain detailed evidence (*e.g.* the words of conversation) a longer period may be accepted (*Richardson* [1971] 2 Q.B. 484). Make a note on your Witness list if the statement was made outside this period. Check that the evidence relates to the date specified in the charge (if it does not, write "Amend charge" on your Notes sheet). Is the layout of the place where the offence allegedly occurred clear? If it is anything other than straightforward, look it up in your street map (Make a note, "Copy street map, page [number]). Do you clearly understand what the witness is describing? (Make a note if you do not.)

As you read, put square brackets round passages of hearsay. On your Witness list, put an "H" against the name of any witness whose statement contains hearsay. If the deletion of the hearsay will cause a problem (for example, that there may be no evidence on an element of the offence), make a note.

Read the rest of the witness statements in the same careful way. Bracket together on your Witness list the names of any two witnesses whose statements are corroborative (against the bracket put "mainly corrob" or "wholly corrob").

If the defendant was questioned, consider what grounds the officer had for suspecting an offence. Should the defendant have been cautioned or arrested? If there might be an objection to the admissibility of that part of the evidence, make a note.

Pause before reading the interview transcript. Decide upon the order in which you will call the witnesses. Generally a loser's statement, if it is to be read, may as well be read first. It is usually best to call the evidence, as far as possible, in chronological order. A witness who either describes the geographical layout or recounts the factual background is often a good opening witness.

Where witnesses are corroborative, aim to take only the best through her/his evidence in full. You can form an impression of how good the witness will be from her/his statement. The more detail s/he noticed the better s/he is likely to be; an ability to describe a layout clearly or a movement accurately is a good sign. Put the names on your Witness list into the order in which you will call them, with "T" against any to be tendered (see page 90).

Onto a treasury tag put in this order: the charge sheet; the "Summary of facts"; and the witness statements, in order. In front of each statement to be read section 9, put the original. Check through the file to ensure there is a certificate of service for each section 9 statement (but leave it where it is in the file). It is of relevance in only two situations. Where a case is being proved in the absence of the defendant the clerk may want confirmation one is on file. Secondly, where a case is adjourned for the maker of a statement to attend court, proof of service may be of relevance to the question of wasted costs. Then edit the interview (see pages 91 to 94).

Preparation of your opening

Prepare an opening for every case you prosecute. On your Opening note against each element of each offence make a note of the evidence.

Example:

Element:	Evidence:
an accident having occurred	Bluebird shunts BMW into Sierra
on a public road	Blackspot Avenue
because of the presence of a car of which he was the driver	Def drove Bluebird index no. T468 WIT
the Def failed to stop	stopped briefly, then drove off

Then read through the "Summary of facts" a second time. Is it accurate? Is there enough detail? Too much? Check the elements of the offence(s). Is there some evidence on each element? Consider how you will "put" your case against each defendant.

Example:

Public Order Act, 1986, s.4—Appleby

used towards another	Walker
threatening behaviour	walking across, rolling up sleeves, shaking fist
intending him to believe unlawful personal violence would be used	
or	
whereby [Walker] likely to believe unlawful personal violence would be used	

Public Order Act, 1986, s. 4—Benson

used towards another	Walker and Young
threatening and abusive words	"You buffoon!", "We'll get you", *etc.*
with intent to provoke immediate unlawful violence	
or	
whereby it was likely such violence would be provoked	

Public Order Act, 1986, s.5—Clarke

used threatening and abusive words	"We'll get you", *etc.*
within the sight and hearing of a person likely to be caused alarm harassment or distress	Young

Prepare a brief note on any term of legal art (for example, "recklessly"), and any relevant legal concept (example: "self-defence").

Consider whether any of the charges are alternatives. As well as obvious ones such as unlawful wounding (section 20) and actual bodily harm (section 47) there are less obvious ones such as failing to comply with an automatic traffic signal and "without due care".

If the allegation involves damage to property or injury, is there a compensation form? If not, make a note. Does the offence involve drugs or weapons? If so, make a note to ask for a destruction order. Finally, read through the items on your Notes sheet. Any matters which were unclear when you first read the statements, but which are now clear can be ticked off. Problems which you cannot now resolve should be copied onto the Witnesses list.

Example:
—Will PC Plod produce the gloves as evidence?
—Copy pp. 9 and 10 of the street plan

Problems requiring thought or legal research should be dealt with now.

Example:
—Can an unreasonable belief one was about to be attacked, support a defence of self-defence?
—At what point did the defendant's acts amount to appropriation of the goods?

The Notes sheet can now be thrown away. Finally add the rest of the papers to your trial bundle so they are in the following order:

—witness list
—charge sheet
—summary of facts
—opening note
—statements in order, with section 9 originals in front of your copies
—interview

—compensation claim form
—previous convictions (form MG16)

If you form the habit of always putting your papers into the same order, you will not have a frantic search whenever you need something unexpectedly.

Now turn to your next case.

OUTSIDE COURT

For all court appearances it is important to arrive early, but particularly when you are prosecuting a session. Open each file in turn. At the front of each trial bundle is the Witness list onto which you have transferred a list of any outstanding tasks. Do any that you can.

Examples:
—Making enlarged copies of the relevant pages of a street map (make six plus one for each defendant)
—Ensuring the cassette player is available if the defence have indicated they want the tape played

Also copy out for the usher a list of the witnesses you expect, by case name. When the witnesses begin to arrive, identify the "officer in the case" for each trial. On your Witness list there may be a number of tasks with which you need her/his assistance. These may include:

—providing the tape of interview (if the defence want it played)
—providing up-to-date previous convictions (form MG16)
—providing any exhibits
—asking one of the witnesses to make a sketch plan of the scene of the incident, for photocopying
—filling in a compensation claim form with a victim of crime

When each civilian witness arrives, thank her/him for coming, and explain the court procedure (see page 25). When the defence advocate arrives:

—ask her/him whether s/he is content to rely on the interview summary or wants the interview tape played (if so, ask the court staff to provide the cassette player)
—ask her/him whether s/he accepts your editing of the interview summary, section 9 statements, and statements of live witnesses
—tell her/him which witnesses you intend to tender

—give her/him copies of any sketches and street plans and ask whether s/he has any objection to their admission
—confirm that the defendant's previous convictions (form MG16) are agreed

Before you go into court check with the usher which witnesses have arrived and mark your list accordingly.

THE PROSECUTION CASE

Opening

Take care with your opening, and the rest of the case will take care of itself. In writing out the elements of each offence, you bring to the forefront of your mind what needs to be proved (including any *mens rea*), and in noting beside each element the evidence on it, you clarify what is the crucial evidence in the case.

In preparing an opening you overview the whole case and as a consequence, will not leave out anything it is necessary to prove, or put in anything unnecessary. First state the allegations in one (usually short) sentence.

Examples:
"The prosecution case is that the defendant stole some groceries from Tesco."

"The prosecution say that the defendant drove too fast, especially around corners, from Wavertree roundabout to Dodderington High Street."

"The prosecution case is that the defendants Mr Hook and Mr Line began a disturbance in a pub, and Mr Sinker, who had not been with them, joined in."

Outline the facts and then relate them to the charges.

Example:
"The lack of due care comprised the excess speed, the lack of signals, and jumping the red light."

Then outline what the prosecution must prove, explaining any legal terms.

Example:
"The prosecution must prove that the [property] belonged to another; that it was damaged; and that the defendant was, at the least, reckless as to whether it was damaged.

" 'Reckless' means that her act created an obvious risk of damage and that she either gave no thought to that risk, or realised there was a risk but went on to do the act, anyway."

Then define any legal concepts upon which you will rely, *e.g.* joint enterprise. If a particular defence, such as self-defence, is indicated in interview, define it, and indicate where the burden of proof lies, and at what standard. Otherwise do not anticipate the defence.

Finally, briefly run through the order of evidence.

Example:

"Ma'am; the prosecution evidence is, firstly, the loser's statement which I shall read. The first live evidence is from the neighbour who saw the attempted break-in; then I shall call both the officers who attended the scene, but I will tender the second of them. Then two of the four officers who arrested the defendant in Grindley Street and, finally, the interviewing officer. Ma'am, with your leave, I shall call the prosecution evidence. I begin by reading..."

In preparing your opening you should decide two matters. Will you open high (giving a detailed outline of the evidence) or low (a bare outline)? The general rule is to open low unless the contrary is indicated; because if you open high and your witnesses do not come up to proof, the defence will claim you have not proved what you set out to prove.

The main reason to open high is that you anticipate a crucial witness will be rather muddled. If you clearly outline what you expect the substance of her/his evidence to be, the magistrates will know what to look out for.

The other main reason for opening high in the magistrates' court is that the opening is your only chance to speak directly to the magistrates. If some detail or details of the evidence are important, it may be well to emphasize them at this stage. If you do not, a skilled defence advocate might concentrate attention somewhere else and the importance of those details will not be fully appreciated.

The other decision is the extent to which, in opening, you should deal with defences which may be open to the defendant. The general rule is not to deal with any defence without good reason. From the papers it may seem obvious that identification will be the issue, but at trial the defendant freely admits her/his presence at the scene and disputes other facts. To have addressed the magistrates on identification will only confuse matters.

The main reasons for dealing in opening with possible defences are these. The defence at the end of the trial may be able to make very persuasive submissions of mixed fact and law. In the magistrates' court you have the right to reply only on the law and, if your opponent has taken care to be accurate on the law, you have no right to reply at all. If you anticipate this happening, it may well be that you would prefer to address the magistrates on the law, or on mixed fact and law, in opening.

The other main reason is that the legal basis of the defence (perhaps a defence of duress) may not be clear to the magistrates until the defendant gives evidence. It may be that the relevant legal concepts (*e.g.* duress) are not clear to the magistrates until the defence advocate makes her/his speech. The effect of this is that as the magistrates heard the prosecution evidence (and perhaps the defence evidence, too) they were not in a position to think: could this amount to duress?

If you anticipate a particular defence will be relied on, ask your opponent. S/he may not tell you. You can then decide whether you think it would be helpful for the magistrates to be aware of that possible defence when they hear the evidence.

If the evidence involves roads, begin with the presumption that a street-plan will be useful and manage without one only if you have decided it is unnecessary. Similarly, begin with the presumption that you need a sketch-plan of the layout of any flat, shop, etc. If the evidence is in any way technical, give a clear explanation or ascertain that the magistrates are familiar with the matter in question.

The opening is the opportunity to create the atmosphere you want. Above all, in opening, strive for clarity. Present the facts in a logical and fluent order, very much as if you were giving a lecture or presentation on a topic on which a clear understanding of the fundamentals is crucial to understanding what follows.

Time spent in preparing an opening is never wasted as it will clarify your thoughts as to the points in issue and how they are to be proved.

Reading evidence section 9

In the Crown Court, whenever you read a statement section 9, use a phrase such as:

Examples:
"Dr Foster's evidence takes the form of a section 9 statement."
"I shall read the supermarket manager's evidence."

The judge will then direct the jury as to the status of section 9 statements. If the statement is the first section 9 statement in the case, introduce it in this way:

Example:
"This is the statement of Mohammed Syed, who made it on the 16th April. He says, 'This statement, consisting of two pages, each signed by me, is true to the best of my knowledge and belief, and I make it knowing that if I have wilfully stated in it anything I know to be false or do not believe to be true I am liable to prosecution', and he has signed that declaration.

"He says, 'I am the owner...'"

Before each section 9 statement you read, the judge will direct the jury as to its status. After the first one, do not read the declaration in full. Use a formula such as:

Example:
"This is the statement of Dr Pavlovski, made on the 4th October. She signed the usual declaration and says this: 'On Tuesday 2nd October...'"

In the magistrates' court, introduce the statement in this way:

Example:
"The first part of the prosecution evidence is a statement which I will read section nine. I hand the original up to your learned clerk. It is the statement of Parminder Khan who made it on the sixteenth of February this year, and signed it."

The statement should be read in full except to exclude hearsay, references to offences which are not before the court, references to bad character and any other irrelevant matters.

Section 10 admissions
A section 10 admission is part of the evidence of the party whose case it assists and should be read by that party (although made by the opposite side). The court has pre-printed forms on which to make such admissions.

Example:
"My friend has kindly admitted certain facts under the provisions of section 10, and I hand the signed form up to your learned clerk. The facts admitted are: that on Tuesday 6th August the defendant was seen by the police doctor who noted the following..."

Examination-in-Chief

Police witnesses
A large proportion of evidence in magistrates' courts is given by police

officers. After you have given the usher the officer's name, give a spare copy of her/his statement to the clerk.

After taking the oath, the officer will identify her/himself ("PC 101 Brown, attached to Beak Street police station, your Worships") and usually ask permission to use her/his notes. If s/he does not, ask her/him whether s/he seeks permission.

Example:

Q. Are there any notes you wish to use to refresh your memory, officer?

A. Yes, please, your Worships.

Q. When were they made?

A. Approximately one hour and twenty minutes after the incident.

Q. Why could you not have made them before then?

A. Because we had to do the booking-in procedure with the prisoners, then attend an accident in a street near the police station.

Q. At the time you made the notes, were the events fresh in your memory?

A. Yes.

Q. Sir, I wonder whether you would give the officer permission to refer to her notes?

In this procedure, the officer will have referred to "the incident" or "the arrest". You can then ask her/him what day it was, what time, where s/he was, whether in uniform/plain clothes, car/foot patrol, etc. Thus, there is no difficulty in "getting started" without leading.

It is frequently difficult to prevent police officers reading more or less word-for-word from their notebooks. While you are still relatively inexperienced, do not worry about that, concentrate on ensuring that none of the evidence is left out, and that all the evidence is clear.

If you have the case well-prepared, ask the defence advocate's permission to lead, up to the point where the evidence becomes contentious (if none of the evidence is, ask to lead it all). In this way you can quickly establish the agreed parts of the evidence and get straight to the part at issue.

Civilian Witnesses

Getting started

It is usually easiest to begin by leaning across to your opponent and asking, "May I lead on time and place?" If the answer is Yes, remember to acknowledge to the magistrates that you are leading.

Example:

"Sir, my friend helpfully allows me to lead; [to the witness:] On March

11th this year, which was a Monday, at about half-past eight in the evening, you were at a window of your house, weren't you?..."

Getting started without leading

There are four stock openings to have at your fingertips:

(i) "In the last [year] have you ever called the police / an ambulance?"

(ii) "In the last [two years] have you ever received treatment / been examined in a hospital?"

(iii) "At any time [this year] have you seen anyone being arrested?"

(iv) "In the last [year] have you ever witnessed / been involved in a traffic accident?"

If any of these questions applies, use it.

Example I:

The witness leaves her flat locked and secure on Friday morning. On her return on Sunday evening, the flat is in disarray with items strewn all about. The lock on a bedroom window is broken.

Q1. In the last year, have you ever called the police?

A. Yes.

Q2. Once or more than once?

A. Once.

Q3. What had happened that made you call the police?

A. The burglary.

Q4. What premises had been burgled?

A. My flat.

Q5. Can you remember on what day of the week you discovered there had been a burglary?

A. It was a Sunday.

Q6. Had you been at home on the previous day, Saturday?

A. No, I was at my parents' over the weekend.

Q7. What day did you leave your flat?

A. Friday.

Q8. What time of day?

A. About ten to eight.

Q9. Ten to eight in the morning or the evening?

A. The morning.

Q10. When you left your flat was it locked or unlocked?

A. Locked.

Q11. When did you next enter your flat?

A. Sunday, at about nine in the evening.

Q12. Was everything the same as you had left it?

All four of the stock opening questions draw the witness's attention to a point of her/his evidence towards the end: in this case, phoning the police. The technique is to get the witness back to the start of her/his evidence without leading, in as few questions as possible. When you use these stock questions for the first time, do not worry if it takes you quite a few questions. Simply concentrate on not leading. Very soon, you will be able to backtrack extremely economically.

Question 2 is asked purely to demonstrate that you are not leading at all, explicitly or implicitly.

It will be noted that the witness is not asked the date of the burglary. Police witnesses virtually always specify the date about which they are giving evidence and, in the rare case when they do not, you should ask. This civilian witness has not been very helpful: the evidence has had to be dragged out of her. If she cannot remember the date of the burglary that may further reduce her confidence. An even less satisfactory possibility is that she might confidently state the wrong date.

One solution is to leave the date to the end of the witness's evidence. By this time she will have spent longer in the witness box and, hopefully, will be more relaxed. You can then ask if she can remember the date:

Example:
Q13.   How often has your flat been burgled in the last year?
A.   Only once.
Q14.   I don't know if you can remember what month it was?

If, in these favourable conditions the witness cannot remember the date, apply for her/him to be shown her/his witness statement, unless it was made too long after the date in question. At this stage your opponent is very likely to lean across to you and say, "Lead on the date".

If the statement cannot be used and the witness cannot remember, there are two ways around the problem. The witness's evidence can be integrated with that of others so that the date can be inferred from the evidence taken together.

Example:
Mr Smith cannot remember the date of the burglary, but it was definitely the Saturday immediately before his wedding anniversary, which he also cannot remember.
Mrs Smith never knew on which date the burglary took place, but remembers perfectly well the date of their wedding.

Alternatively, it may be possible to elicit other evidence from the witness so that the details s/he cannot remember are not needed. This has been done in the example above. At question 13 the witness says her flat has been burgled only once in the previous year, so the evidence she has given about that burglary must relate to any other evidence of a burglary at that address in that year. The rest of the evidence (for example, from the police) which connects the defendant to the burglary, will sufficiently indicate the date.

Example II:

Q1. In the last year, have you ever called the police?

A. Yes.

Q2. Once or more than once?

A. At least five times.

Q3. [To magistrate:] Sir, would you excuse me one moment while I look at this document?

Q4. [To witness:] For what reasons did you have to call the police those five times?

A. I got home from work in February. I'd been kept late because the oxidiser had been jamming due to the wrong grade of oil having been delivered by—

Q5. I apologise for interrupting you, Mr Bloggins, but could you just tell us very briefly why you phoned the police?

A. To report my car stolen.

Q6. And the second time, why did you phone the police?

A. From my bedroom window, I—

Q7. I'm sorry, Mr Bloggins. Very briefly, what had you seen?

A. Boy pinching apples.

Q8. And the third call, what had you seen?

A. Four cars, parked in residents' parking spaces, they were no more resi—

Q9. And the fourth call, Mr Bloggins, what had you seen?

A. I didn't see anything. I heard. I was sitting in my front room, it was about the middle of the afternoon and I was just finishing the 'Daily Express' crossword...

In this example, the stock question has not worked. The average person, in the witness-box, primed to give her/his evidence about a traffic accident, when asked, "Have you called the police in the last year? More than once?" will reply, "Only once that I remember", forgetting any other calls made about other matters. This witness makes the disconcerting reply, "At least five times".

Whenever, in examination-in-chief, you receive a reply which throws you off-balance, give no sign of surprise, but, as at question 3, ask for time to read documents, examine exhibits, or whatever. If you speak very confidently and matter-of-factly, the magistrates will be unaware of your surprise at the answer.

It will be noted that questions 8 and 9 are slightly leading in that the witness may have phoned the police for a reason other than that he had seen something. If there is any objection, the question can easily be replaced with the previous "For what reason did you call the police?".

Advocates object to leading for two reasons: to see whether, without assistance, the witness is able to remember the evidence; and because they think a strict prohibition on leading may throw their opponent off-balance. In this example, the witness clearly has total recall and the advocate manages without leading effortlessly. Most advocates in these circumstances would, at about question 8, simply invite you to lead.

Most civilian prosecution witnesses are victims or losers or observers of events which have lead up to an arrest, so it is rare for none of the stock openings to apply. The likelihood of having such a witness and also an opponent who will allow no leading is therefore very small. If all else fails, you can begin in this way:

Example:
Q1.   When you were sitting outside the courtroom, you were shown a statement you had made, weren't you?
A.   Yes.
Q2.   Was the statement about something you had witnessed?
A.   Yes.
Q3.   Were you indoors or outdoors when you witnessed it?
A.   Outdoors.
Q4.   Where?
A.   In Elmtree Road.
Q5.   Why were you in Elmtree Road?
A.   I'd collected a takeaway from the Chinese restaurant.
Q6.   On foot or by vehicle?
Q.   About what time of day was this?
Q.   Were you alone or with anyone else?

Questions 1 and 2 are, of course, leading but unobjectionable as they do not suggest anything material. It is sometimes said that when one is prohibited from leading, a useful opening question is: "What have you come to court to give evidence about?", but it is unsatisfactory at two levels. At an informational level it may well yield an unhelpful answer. For example, a witness who has seen a suspect interfere with a motor vehicle, for which he is being tried, and on arrest assault a policeman, to which he has pleaded Guilty (so it is kept off the court register), may answer: "That (pointing) young man assaulting a policeman".

More importantly, the question leaves everything to the witness, giving her/him no help, so s/he begins her/his evidence feeling unsure of her/himself and probably giving rather tentative answers. Because the opening questions above are entirely leading, they are easy for the witness. The answers can be built onto with short questions ("Where were you?, When had you arrived there?, Which room were you in?")

which the witness can answer confidently, and then one can move imperceptibly on to the narrative part of the evidence.

With a prosecution witness it is generally inappropriate to begin examination-in-chief with questions to put the witness at ease ("What work do you do?, How long have you done it?"). All the court wants to know is what s/he saw and heard on the day. As you have to go straight to the point, it is easiest for the witness if you guide her/him firmly.

Civilian evidence

The two helpful maxims about eliciting civilian evidence are mutually contradictory. One is, "Keep the witness on a tight rein", and the other is, "Let the witness tell her/his own story." Both have their place.

Keeping a tight rein

A rule which it is only very rarely safe to break is "Never expect any help from a witness". It is your task and responsibility to elicit from the witness the evidence s/he has to give, and two dangers are that s/he may get parts of her/his evidence confused, or worse still, forget it altogether.

If you make the witness stick to her/his statement which s/he has read through several times before coming into court, the familiarity of the sequence will assist her/his recall. It will incidentally make sure that any details which are crucial are included in the evidence the witness gives, and the tight rein prevents digression.

Because you are controlling the evidence, you can ensure its orderly and logical presentation which will assist the tribunal. You can also pace it, to make it easy to take notes.

A witness is kept on a tight rein by the use of leading and prompting questions. While the usher is bringing the witness into court, lean across to your opponent and ask: "Can I lead up to... [wherever the evidence becomes contentious]?"

Begin in a friendly but authoritative manner with a question which is both completely leading, but also easy.

Example:

"You saw a fight in the 'Bucket and Spade' pub, didn't you?"

Avoid a question which, although leading, is not easy.

Example:

"You saw a fight in the 'Bucket and Spade' pub on the 17th March, didn't you?"

Whether or not the witness has a clear memory of the date, this question quite unnecessarily introduces a potential difficulty.

Example:
"Do you remember something which happened on 17th March?"

This question pointlessly combines a large element of leading and minimal help to the witness.
You might continue:

Q2.   You had arrived at the pub at about 8 p.m., hadn't you?
A.   Yes.
Q3.   Were you alone?
A.   I was with my wife.
Q4.   Will you look at the sketch plan? Take a minute or two to get your bearings. Can you point on the plan to whereabouts you were sitting?
A.   About there. [Points]
Q5.   In which direction were you facing?
A.   More or less towards the bar.
Q6.   And your wife?
A.   More or less to this side.
Q7.   Did you have a clear view of the bar area or were there obstructions?
A.   I had a clear view.
Q8.   Before you came into the "Bucket and Spade" had you had any alcoholic drink?
A.   No.
Q9.   At lunchtime?
A.   No.
Q10.   The fight broke out at about 9.45, didn't it?
A.   Yes.
Q11.   Between 8 p.m. and 9.45, what did you drink?
A.   I was on my fourth pint when the fight started, but I hadn't drunk much of it.
Q12.   Pints of what?
A.   Guinness.

Only three of these questions are leading. If leading were prohibited, you might have begun:

Q.   At any time this year, have you seen an arrest being made?
A.   Yes.
Q.   One arrest or more than one?
A.   Just the one.
Q.   Where was it made?
A.   At the "Bucket and Spade".
Q.   What sort of premises are the "Bucket and Spade"?

A. It's a pub.

Q. Can you remember what time you arrived at the "Bucket and Spade"?

A. Not really, some time in the evening, between, say, half-past seven and half-past eight.

Q. Were you alone?...

If none of the evidence is contentious, it is possible to lead much more.

Example:

Q. You saw a fight in the "Bucket and Spade" pub, didn't you?

A. Yes.

Q. There is no dispute about the date. Do you accept it was 6th March this year?

A. Yes.

Q. You arrived at that pub with your wife at about 8 o'clock, didn't you?

A. Yes.

Q. And, if you would look at the sketch plan, you were sitting there, weren't you, where it is marked "H", and your wife was sitting where it is marked "W", wasn't she?

A. Yes, that's right.

Q. There was nothing obstructing your view of the whole bar area, was there?

A. No.

Q. When you arrived at the pub you were entirely sober and...

With police witnesses, it is often time-saving to lead evidence completely in this way. With civilian witnesses there are three reasons why it is generally better to lead only partially, as in the first example. Most importantly, the witness gets used to speaking in court. Secondly, there is a greater sense of the reality of the evidence if the details are filled in by the witness. And thirdly, partial leading is inherently more interesting to listen to than a succession of "yes"s from the witness.

Once you have arrived at the contentious part of the evidence you must, of course, stop leading but, having set the scene, you would not, in any case, wish to lead: you simply continue asking prompting questions. Always stick closely to the sequence and language of the witness statement.

When the matters in issue have been covered, lean over to your opponent and ask: shall I lead her/him to the end? The usual answer is Yes.

Example:

Q. [to magistrate:] Sir, with my friend's permission I intend to lead Mr Wilkinson to the end of his evidence. [To witness:] It's right, isn't it, that the police left at about twenty to eleven?

A. Yes.

Q. You bought yourself a further pint of Guinness and your wife a vodka and lemonade and, after consuming those drinks, you left the pub at about eleven-fifteen?

A. Yes.

Q. The next day a police officer came round to your house in the evening and you made a statement which he wrote down and you signed, is that right?

A. It is.

Q. Was your wife present when you gave your statement?

A. She was not.

Q. Were you present at any time when she made a statement?

A. I was in the house, but not in the same room.

Q. Thank you, would you stay there, please, for some questions from this lady.

The technique for keeping a witness on a tight rein is as follows. Lead as much of the evidence as you are allowed, except to let the witness "fill in the details" with short answers. ("What were you drinking?...Guinness".) Stick closely to the witness statement (to assist the witness's memory). Elicit each fact in the statement by means of a prompting question (see page 82, questions 3–9). When a fact does not follow sequentially from the previous one (e.g. "suddenly I noticed a handkerchief..."), elicit the evidence up to that point, and then use a prompting question ("Did you notice anything?") Always echo the wording of the statement ("noticed/notice").

Telling her/his own story

The advantages of the witness "telling her/his own story" is that the evidence is more authentic, because it comes directly from the witness; more vivid, because it is expressed in her/his words; and more interesting because it is an unbroken narrative.

Only if the witness's evidence is quite short should you let her/him tell her/his own story immediately after s/he has taken the oath and identified her/himself. In any other case you should lead or prompt the evidence up to the contentious part.

If you are allowed to lead, begin with entirely leading questions and then allow the witness to "fill in the colours" to assist her/his recollection and get used to speaking in court. If you are prohibited from leading, use a series of forced-choice questions to get the witness to the starting point of her/his evidence, and then ask probing questions (see page 101) to "fill in the details".

During this opening part of the evidence take the opportunity to remind the witness to speak loudly; and explain that the evidence should be given sufficiently slowly for notes to be taken. Take the witness right to the point from which you want her/him to give her/his own evidence. Ask a forced-choice question which allows a longer answer, then ask a relatively open question.

Example:
Q1. Did any particular voices attract your attention?
A. Not until the ruck started.
Q2. What voices attracted your attention then?
A. A fellow I know, Edward Potter, was in an argument with a short fellow I had never seen before.
Q3. Could you hear what the argument was about?
A. All I could hear was Edward Potter saying...

Question 2 is still directing the witness to give the evidence you want, but question 3 follows the lead taken by the witness.

Example:
Q1. Was there any traffic in the opposite direction?
A. Yes.
Q2. Did you notice any vehicle in particular?
A. Yes.
Q3 What vehicle was it?
A. A Ford Escort.
Q4. How far away from you was it when you first noticed it?
A. About 600 metres.
Q5. What attracted your attention to it?
A. It was moving into my lane.
Q6. Did you do anything?
A. At first, I thought, maybe he is...

Questions 3 and 4 direct the witness; question 5 begins to allow the witness to tell her/his own story, and question 6 invites the witness to continue the account.

Once the witness has begun to tell the story, you should act only as the magistrates' mouthpiece. If the witness is going too fast, say, "Pause there", then invite her/him to resume, with "Yes?" or "You were telling us?". If s/he persistently goes too fast, say, "Watch the clerk's pen". If the witness's account begs a questions, ask it.

If the witness stops in her/his account, prompt her/him in the least obtrusive way ("Yes?" or "Go on" are less noticeable than "What happened next?" or "And then what?"). As far as possible prompt by gesture and expression rather than words. The magistrates' attention should be entirely focused on the witness; the less aware they are of you the better.

There will usually be one or two questions arising from the witness's evidence which you refrained from asking so as not to interrupt the narrative flow. Ask those questions when the witness has finished her/his account, then obtain your opponent's permission and lead the witness to the end of her/his evidence, as at pages 83 to 84.

Choosing Which Technique

It is obviously possible to conduct an examination-in-chief which is a compromise between the two approaches. Indeed, the vast majority of examinations in court combine elements of both.

What is important is that whenever you are examining in chief, you are aware of the technique you are using, and have deliberately chosen it to meet the needs of that particular part of that examination. To demonstrate the two techniques, they have been presented above in forms more extreme than you would normally encounter in court. In any actual examination you will vary your questioning along the continuum between keeping a tight rein and completely giving the witness her/his head.

Keeping the witness on a tight rein is recommended where:

—the evidence is long
—the evidence is complicated
—the evidence is technical
—the evidence is not disputed (one is only not leading to let the witness practise speaking)
—the witness is nervous
—the witness has a poor memory

Letting the witness tell her/his own story is recommended where:

—the evidence is short
—the evidence is uncomplicated
—it is apparent that the witness has a clear recollection of the events
—the credibility (not content) of the evidence is important (i.e. where "it's one person's word against another")

The typical overall pattern of an examination-in-chief is that one generally begins by keeping a tight rein, relaxes it as appropriate then, the contentious evidence over, one leads the witness to the end.

Defence Cross-Examination

In most cases you will be able to anticipate the defence case. Even if it is not spelt out in interview, there are only a limited number of defences to most charges, (*e.g.* in assault cases, self-defence; in shop-lifting, genuine mistake; in public order, that the words were not said).

But the defence cross-examination of the prosecution evidence is the first time you hear the defence "put". Make sure the questioning is slow enough for you to take an adequate note. Lean across to your opponent and ask her/him to take it more slowly. If, after doing this twice, it is still too fast, explain to the magistrates you are having difficulty keeping up.

Note the evidence only on the left-hand pages of your notebook, leaving the right side free for later notes. Adopt a symbol to indicate questions which put the defence case, and indicate the witness's agreement or disagreement with a tick or a cross.

Example:
> How close were you when P hit F? – very
> < He hit him only once?—✗ twice
> < He immediately moved back?—✗
> T then stepped between them?—√

Make notes of:
(a) whatever is asked (or not asked) about each element of each offence, *e.g.*, if you are prosecuting a case of careless driving which involves an allegation of excess speed, and the cross-examiner does not ask the witness about that, note, "Speed not challenged"
(b) the case which is "put" by the cross-examiner. Here the words of the questioner are more important than the answers (which will often be blanket denials). Any agreement by the witness will be important to note
(c) any challenges to the prosecution evidence
(d) any new evidence mentioned by the defence, *e.g.* "Did you notice a youth sitting on a wall on the opposite side of the road?"
By the end of the cross-examination of the prosecution's first witness to fact, the nature of the defence will usually be clear. If it is, make sure that you understand the detail, *e.g.* precisely what the defendant is said to have done in self-defence. If you are unsure, indicate this to the magistrates when you rise to re-examine (example: "It is not clear to me, ma'am, whether or not PC Scott's evidence about the window is accepted").

If the defence is not clear, there are three main possibilities. Firstly, that the defence advocate has neglected to put her/his case. Secondly, that there is an essentially technical defence which you have overlooked. Thirdly, that the defence is one which is dependent on defence evidence, *e.g.* duress.

If you suspect the defence may be one dependent on defence evidence, it may be prudent to ask your witnesses to remain in the court building in case you want to recall them to give evidence in rebuttal.

If your opponent has neglected to put her/his case, there is nothing you can, or need, do. It will usually be worth running through in your mind the elements of the offences to ensure there is evidence on each, and also checking that the allegations in the summons are consistent with the evidence. If you discover a discrepancy, apply to amend the information.

Examples:
—A car number is wrongly given
—Threatening words and behaviour are specified in the summons, whereas the evidence is of abusive and insulting words
—The date of the offence is wrongly given

At the first convenient opportunity (for example, between witnesses) ask the magistrates to excuse you for a moment and inform your opponent of the application you are about to make, and then apply to amend.

Example:
"May it please you, ma'am; at this stage it is my application to amend the information. For the word 'seventh' in 'seventh of July' I apply to substitute 'ninth'.
"As you will have appreciated from the evidence of the first two witnesses, the prosecution allege that this offence occurred on the ninth of July. I apologise to the court and to my friend for not having noticed the mistake earlier."

Magistrates have wide powers to amend the information at any stage in the trial. By the Magistrates Courts Act 1980, s.123(1) minor discrepancies between the evidence and the information do not require amendment. However, if the defendant is present it is always prudent to seek to amend the information to reflect the prosecution case.

If the discrepancy is such as to mislead the defendant s/he is entitled (by Magistrates' Courts Act 1980, s.123(2)) to an adjournment.

Re-examination
You will want to re-examine in two main situations: when your opponent has elicited evidence which would have a different effect seen in context; and when you know the witness could give further evidence which would

explain or support evidence s/he has given, or would refute a suggestion made to her/him.

As you will not want to re-examine on anything non-contentious, it follows that in re-examination you will hardly ever be allowed to lead.

You should not go over ground already covered in chief. It is therefore usually easiest to start with a reference to the cross-examination.

Example I:
The witness has given evidence under cross-examination that the complainant had admitted hitting the defendant.
Q. You said the complainant had admitted having hit the defendant.
A. Yes.
Q. Did he say why he had done so?
A. In self-defence, because the defendant was throwing punches at him.

Example II:
Q. You said in answer to my friend, that you saw the boys throwing stones at the garage doors?
A. Yes.
Q. Do you know whether any damage was done to the doors?
A. Yes, there were dents.
Q. How do you know that?
A. I saw them.
Q. When?
A. I went to look at them as soon as I'd chased the boys away.
Q. How do you know the dents had not been there previously?
A. I'd closed my own door only an hour before and it was in perfect condition then.

Example III:
Q. It was suggested to you that the boy PC Crisp arrested in Hardy Street might not have been the boy you had chased into that street. Were there many people about in that street?
A. There was no-one. It was four o'clock in the morning.

As a rule of thumb, until you have gained experience it is prudent to re-examine only when you are clear that the witness has evidence s/he can give which would bolster or put much more in context her/his previous testimony and that the additional evidence is on a point of significance.

Releasing witnesses

At the end of re-examination give the court the opportunity of putting questions.

Examples:
"There is nothing else in re-examination. I don't know whether the
bench has any questions for this witness?"
"There is no re-examination. I wonder, sir, whether you have any
questions for the witness?"

After any questions from the bench, ask your opponent whether s/he
wants to ask anything arising from them, then ask for the witness to be
released.

Example:
"May the witness be released, sir?"

Tendering witnesses
When two police officers give effectively the same evidence but each gives
some necessary evidence which the other does not, (with permission) lead
the second officer through a very abbreviated account of the common
evidence and then take her/him through the evidence only s/he can give,
leading if allowed.

Example:
Q. And while PC Khan arrested the first defendant, is it right that
    you arrested and cautioned the second defendant at 2.19 p.m.?
A. Yes.
Q. What was his reply to caution?
A. "You must be joking."

If all the evidence is common to both officers, ask your opponent whether
s/he wants to ask the second any questions. If not, do not call her/him.

If your opponent does want the second officer called, tender her/him.
There is no set formula for doing this, but it will assist the magistrates
to know how s/he fits into the prosecution case.

Example:
Q.   [to magistrate:] May he use those notes, sir?
Mag. Yes.
Q.   [to witness:] Officer, I'm not going to ask you to give your
      evidence in full. It is right, isn't it, that on Tuesday, 24th
      October last year at about 3 p.m. you were on duty with PC
      Baines in the Paradise Shopping Centre?
A.   Yes I was.
Q.   You were present at 3.17 p.m. when he arrested Mark Fisher?
A.   Yes I was.
Q.   Would you remain there?

Interviews

Edit the interview summary by placing square brackets around the excluded parts. Exclude:

(a) any question the content of which you cannot prove

Example I:
Q1.   One of the neighbours has given a statement that he saw you damage the Sierra.
A.   No comment.

Unless you call the neighbour to give evidence you should exclude this question. If the answer has evidential value, it should be given and the question can be summarised rather than given verbatim.

Example:
Q2.   One of the neighbours has given a statement that he saw you damage the Sierra.
A.   At the time you mentioned I was playing pool with my brother-in-law in the "Pie and Pelican".

This can be given:

"It was put to the defendant that he had damaged the Sierra and he replied, 'At the time you mentioned I was playing pool with my brother-in-law in the "Pie and Pelican".'"

The answer has evidential value because the defendant is claiming an alibi. It may assist the defendant. He may intend to call his brother-in-law to prove he was elsewhere, and the answer will show this is not a recent fabrication.

It may harm the defendant. The prosecution may intend to call the landlord of the "Pie and Pelican" to prove the pub was closed for redecoration in the relevant week. The answer has inherent evidential value whether it assists either or neither party.

If the answer has no independent evidential value and the question is objectionable (as question 1 above) both question and answer should be excluded.

(b) questions dealing with other allegations
Exceptionally, an answer may have relevance to the charge before the court.

Example II:
The defendant was arrested for taking a conveyance without the

owner's consent and is additionally charged with driving without due care. He has pleaded Guilty to the taking without consent, which has been left off the court's register.

In answer to questions about the taking without consent, the defendant gave a detailed account of his movements that evening which is relevant to the driving without due care charge.

The questions should be summarised to exclude references to the taking without consent, and the answers given verbatim (minus any necessary omissions) as in Example I above.

Alternatively, your opponent may prefer to make a section 10 admission (see page 75) to obviate your presenting that evidence.

(c) questions revealing bad character

If the answer is of evidential value, the question should be summarised to exclude reference to bad character and the answer given verbatim (with any necessary omissions) as in Example I above.

(d) answers revealing bad character

If an answer which reveals bad character is evidentially valuable, you are entitled to include it: it is for the defence to ask the court to rule it inadmissible.

Example:
Q1.   Why did you think they might be stolen goods?
A.   Because I've bought stolen goods from him before.
Q2.   Knowing they were stolen?
A.   Yes.

Answer 1 clearly has probative value because it tends to show the defendant had good grounds for belief (not mere fanciful suspicion) that the goods were stolen. You are entitled to include question and answer 1 unless your opponent objects and seeks a ruling.

Question 2 is clearly inadmissible because all that is relevant to the present charge is that the defendant knew the seller to be a handler (it makes no difference when s/he learned this). Question 2 shows only that in the past the defendant had committed an offence.

The obvious problem with forcing the defence to seek a ruling on admissibility is that the magistrates will in any case hear the evidence objected to.

The argument against voluntarily excluding question and answer 1 is that it is not easy to prove the state of a person's belief, and the defendant's admission s/he knew the seller to be a handler is of such relevance that the magistrates would be prevented from making a fair decision if kept in ignorance of it.

The argument for excluding it is that the defendant has in any case admitted s/he thought the goods might be stolen and that, taken together with the circumstances of the sale and the price, is a strong case against her/him.

This is a borderline case. It will generally be right to exclude any answer revealing bad character (unless it is an element of the present offence, such as driving while disqualified).

In presenting an interview you should indicate to the magistrates whether the evidence is a transcript or a summary or a mixture of the two. It will usually be possible to edit a transcript by simply excluding certain words. If that cannot be done, summarise instead. You must not add words to a transcript.

Example:

Q. Then what did you do?

A. I gave him a slapping, like I did last year.

Q. What were the injuries when you attacked him last year?

A. Three broken ribs, black eye; this time I only warned him, I just bust his jaw.

Q. Both last year and this time you threatened him with a knife, didn't you?

A. Not this time.

becomes:

Q. Then what did you do?

A. I gave him a slapping, [like I did last year.

Q. What were the injuries when you attacked him last year?

A. Three broken ribs, black eye; this time] I only warned him, I just bust his jaw.

Q. [Both last year and this time you threatened him with a knife, didn't you? } summarise

A. Not this time.]

and reads:

"I said: 'Then what did you do?'. Reply: 'I gave him a slapping. I only warned him, I just bust his jaw.' It was put to the defendant that he had threatened the Victim with a knife, and he denied it."

If the interview is short and the defence advocate does not want to question the interviewing officer, with defence agreement you can read the interview by way of section 9 (see page 74) or, if the original is not to hand, a section 10 admission (see page 75).

If the officer is called and the interview is short, s/he can read it all. You may prefer to split up a longer interview so that the officer gives the interviewee's replies (which are the evidence) and you read the rest. The advantages are that it makes it clearer who said what; it is more interesting to listen to; and you may be better at pacing the reading than the officer.

If you have voluntarily excluded part of the interview, you cannot put it to the defendant in cross-examination as an inconsistent statement, but you can use the information contained as the basis for a question.

Example:
In interview:
Q.   Why did you think they might be stolen goods?
A.   Because I've bought stolen goods from him before.

In cross-examination:
Q1.   You said in interview you thought they might be stolen goods.
A.   I said I thought they might be. I didn't think they were.
Q2.   Why did you think they might be stolen?
A.   I didn't think they were. I just thought they were very cheap. One possibility was they might be stolen, that's all.
Q3.   You actually knew that the man who sold them does sell stolen goods, didn't you?
A.   I had no reason to think that.
Q4a.   That's not what you told the police, is it?
or:
Q4b.   Haven't you said you knew the seller had sold stolen goods in the past?

Question 4 in either form is improper. You are entitled to ask question 3. The defendant may be surprised into answering "yes". If s/he answers negatively, you cannot take this line of questioning any further.

When the magistrates give permission for your last witness to be released, use a formula such as: "Thank you, ma'am, that is the prosecution case."

Submission of No Case

If the basis of the submission is that the evidence on one element was inadequate and the only witness on that element quite clearly did not come up to proof, you should concede that the charge should be dismissed.

Example:
Witness statement:
"The driver was Errol Benskin."

Witness:
"The driver I thought was Errol Benskin, but, having thought about it, I'm not sure."

If the submission is that there is no evidence of the appropriate *mens rea*, your Opening Note enables you to reply quite briefly.

Example:
"May it please you, ma'am; you will remember that I said in opening that the prosecution case is that you can properly infer that the defendant must have believed the video recorder was stolen from the price, and from the fact that, even on her account, which the prosecution does not accept, it was offered for sale by a complete stranger who drew his car up next to the defendant, who bought the video recorder without even making sure it worked."

Generally if the submission is that the prosecution evidence is so vague or inconsistent that it cannot found a safe conviction, there is no point in seeking to reply to the submission. If the court requires persuasion that there is a *prima facie* case, the evidence is clearly very weak. A possible exception is where you feel the weaknesses of the prosecution evidence were more apparent than real and that the case is such that the defendant will have to give evidence.

THE DEFENCE CASE

Defendant's Evidence-in-Chief

Ensure that the evidence is given slowly enough for you to take an adequate note and in particular take a full note of the defendant's evidence on:

—each element of the offence
—anything upon which the defendant relies as a defence
—any part of the prosecution case which was challenged

If you think the defence will or may call corroborative evidence, take accurate notes of the evidence on the surrounding circumstances (see page 103).

As far as possible, be aware of the manner in which the defendant gives her/his evidence. It is often said that the advocate should completely concentrate on the witness as s/he gives her/his evidence. While this is wise advice, in one's early trials it is more realistic to concentrate on taking an adequate note of the evidence and being clear on the details of the defence.

Cross-examination of the Defendant

In the model cross-examination, the advocate asks the defendant a series of difficult questions rather quickly. The defendant contradicts her/himself hopelessly, falls into traps cleverly set by the advocate, and ends up by making a full confession of guilt.

Because series of difficult questions and cleverly-set traps are hard to devise, some prosecutors fall back on the expedient of going over again the ground covered in evidence-in-chief, but putting the questions with a sneer, and throwing in a few accusations of lying.

Do not attempt to ask questions in rapid succession. This is a useful technique, but only in certain limited situations (see page 101). As a general approach it is counter-productive (the magistrates become confused sooner than the defendant).

Approach the cross-examination of a defendant in this way. Be clear what the prosecution case is. In some cases it is known in detail what is alleged against the defendant (for example, in an assault case, where the prosecution witnesses saw, or received, the attack). Other cases are largely inferential (for example, in a fraudulent tax disc case, the prosecution have no means of knowing how the defendant came by the disc).

There are generally three aims in the cross-examination of a defendant: to discredit at least parts of her/his evidence; to elicit further evidence from her/him which assists the prosecution case; and the obligatory putting of the prosecution case.

It is unusual to elicit much helpful evidence from a defendant; the principal aim is generally to discredit at least part of her/his case. Avoid a spatter-gun approach, in which you challenge all of the evidence simply because it came from the defendant. Such an approach is frequently offensive and always less than maximally effective.

At this point the magistrates have heard the prosecution and defence accounts of what happened. Jot down your "argument" that the defendant is guilty.

Example:
Prosecution evidence:
The defendant is seen in a supermarket "furtively" slipping items into his own bag; he pays for the items in the wire basket; on arrest before leaving the shop he says, "I must have put them in my bag by mistake."

Defence evidence:
The defendant is on tranquillisers for personal problems; he had put the items in his bag by mistake.

Argument:

Point 1: the defendant was seen to look round "furtively" before slipping items into his bag

Point 2: The items in his bag are significantly more expensive than those in the basket

Point 3: Why take a shopping bag into the supermarket, and then carry away the shopping in the supermarket's carrier-bag?

Point 4: One would expect a genuinely-mistaken customer to be more upset at being stopped than the defendant was.

Usually it will be clear from the defendant's evidence exactly what her/his case is. In the exceptional case in which questions are raised in the hearer's mind, it will generally be best to put those questions to the defendant straightaway. That will clarify the defence case to you at the beginning, and make the magistrates feel you and they are on the same wavelength.

Once part of her/his evidence has been challenged, a defendant will naturally be less well-disposed towards the cross-examiner, so it is generally easier to begin the cross-examination on topics on which you accept, in the main, what the defendant has said, or on which you are at least neutral.

Example:

Point 1 involves a direct challenge to the evidence about the manner in which the defendant took the goods, whereas no challenge is involved in point 2, as the prices of the goods are indisputable.

Point 3 involves much conjecture: if the defendant were only shopping at the supermarket it seems odd to take a shopping-bag and not use it. However if he intended shopping elsewhere too it may have been quite natural to take a bag. The prosecution hypothesis is that this was a deliberate shop-lifting trip and the bag was an essential part of it. Unconvincing evidence on this point from the defendant could be important, but it will be easy for the defendant to give a plausible explanation.

Point 4 requires further evidence from the defendant, but does not necessitate any challenges by the prosecution.

Because it does not involve challenge to the defendant's evidence, and deals with an early stage of the story, it is best to begin with point 3.

Having decided upon your first topic, be clear about your objectives.

Example:

Point 3 is speculative. The prosecution case is that the defendant has set out quite deliberately to steal from the supermarket and had needed to take a bag to put the stolen goods into. The objective is to catch the defendant off-guard and see if he admits intending to shop only at the supermarket. Obviously, if the defendant realises the point of the questions he may tailor his evidence to deal with it.

Q1. You arrived at the supermarket at about ten past ten, didn't you?

A.   Yes.

Q2. Had you come from home or elsewhere?

A.   Home.

Q3. And you had been into several other shops before entering the supermarket?

A.   No, I hadn't.

Q4. Well, you had intended to visit other shops on your way home, didn't you?

A.   No. I was only going to take my shopping home.

With these four questions, it has been established that the defendant claims to have left home intending to visit only the supermarket before returning home. The advocate knows that the defendant had not previously done any shopping because on arrest the only items found in the shopping bag were those allegedly stolen.

If the witness had answered either that he had already visited, or had intended afterwards to visit, other shops, point 3 would have to be abandoned. But the questioning would simply continue smoothly onto the next topic without any harm being done to the prosecution case; and without anyone except the prosecutor being aware of the point s/he had been trying to get evidence for. In this instance, the answers are favourable to the prosecution. They are mentally noted for later use.

The next point in the prosecution argument is point 1, that the defendant looked around "furtively" before placing the goods in his bag. Almost every case involves this sort of conflict of evidence about detail, where the fundamentals (the fact that the goods were put into the bag) are agreed.

If the alternative version is put directly to the defendant, he is likely to be able to explain it away.

Example:

Q5a. Isn't it right that you picked up the tin of ham, looked round to see if anyone was watching you, and then slipped it into your bag?

A.   I do remember looking round. I picked up the ham which I had intended to buy for when my family came round on Sunday. It was quite expensive, so I looked round to see what other brands there were, or whether there was something cheaper that would do, such as corned beef. I was going through the alternatives in my mind. I think that's why I put it in the wrong bag.

In dealing with conflicts of evidence, always think argumentatively. It is the defendant's case that he was largely unaware of what he was doing. This could be challenged.

Example:
Q. You were perfectly aware of what you were doing, weren't you?
A. No; I hardly knew what I was doing.

If the defendant commits himself to the position that he was unaware of what he was doing, he can be confronted with the store detective's evidence.

Example:
Q. You heard the evidence of the store detective, didn't you?
Q. Do you know where she was watching you from?
Q. Have you any reason to doubt her evidence that she saw you clearly?
Q. You waited until no-one was near you, didn't you?

It would be difficult for an untruthful witness to steer a course between on the one hand, accepting the prosecution evidence and, on the other hand, by disputing it, conceding that he was aware of what he was doing.

The fourth point, that an innocent shopper would be more upset than the defendant appeared to be, is a difficult one. People react very differently. If the advocate states affirmatively "A wrongly accused person would react in x way", a magistrate is quite likely to think, "I wouldn't".

Again, be clear about your objectives.

Example:
Having heard the defendant's evidence-in-chief, you feel his reaction to accusation was that of an habitual shop-lifter (which you know he is) rather than an innocent, but forgetful, shopper accused for the first time.

The evidence needs testing very gently.

Example:
Q. How well do you remember the moment when the security guard stopped you?

If the answer to this rings false, leave it there. You have enough, and any more questions may enable the defendant to improve his position.

If the answer suggests guilt ("I felt like a criminal") you could ask:

Q. Why did you think he was stopping you?

A. I didn't know.

Q. I suggest you felt guilty for the obvious reason: you knew you had several items in your bag which you had not paid for?

If the advocate gently probes what happened between the defendant being stopped and being taken to the police station, it may be that the only thing which will be established is that the defendant said very little: but this may be a point in the prosecution's favour in that when people find themselves in a compromising position the usual tendency is to say a great deal in explanation and apology.

The second point (the stolen goods were the more expensive ones) is the best point to finish with as the objective facts are so strong against the defendant.

Example:

Q1. Let's go through all seventeen items from the most expensive to the cheapest: the salmon steaks, price £-, not paid for; the ham, price £-, not paid for; the ..., etc.
The most expensive items you didn't pay for, did you?

A. What about the washing powder? That was expensive.

Q2. It was too bulky to slip into your bag, wasn't it?

A. I didn't deliberately put anything into my bag.

Q3. The only other expensive item which you paid for was the chicken. That could not easily be slipped into a bag, could it?

A. I only put things into my bag by mistake.

Q4. Are you saying it is purely a coincidence that you made a mistake with every single item that was both small and expensive?

A. I didn't intend to take anything without paying.

This procedure is the most effective way to demonstrate that the items the defendant had not paid for were the most expensive. A more precise way of putting it would be to compare the average prices of the paid-for and unpaid-for items. This is not sufficiently concrete for the non-statistically minded, who might think it could be "just coincidence". The fact that nearly all the items at the top of the list were not paid for, and all the items at the bottom of the list were, is very clear.

If the defendant had not raised the matter of the two expensive but paid-for items, the advocate would have done. It is more effective when raised by the defendant. Questions 2 and 3 are very difficult for the defendant. They beg a Yes or No answer, but cannot be satisfactorily (from the defendant's point of view) answered either Yes or No.

Discrediting the Defendant

In almost all cases it is implicit in the prosecution case that part of the defendant's evidence is lies. Never impugn evidence for the sake of it: only if it is a necessary part of your case that certain evidence is untruthful.

Be clear about your objective. Almost never will you be in a position mathematically to prove the defendant is lying. Hardly ever will s/he break down and confess her/his guilt. Your aim is not to have and win an argument with the defendant. It is to put such questions to her/him that her/his evidence is disbelieved. This is sometimes because it is self-contradictory, but much more usually because the manner in which it is given makes the tribunal feel sure that it is untrue. Sometimes when a defendant hesitates before answering a question, it is clear s/he is working out the most favourable answer. Or it may be clear s/he is taking refuge behind a wall of "I can't remember"'s.

The basic approach in all cross-examination is argumentative: "the prosecution version is to be preferred because..." But there are several techniques specifically for discrediting evidence.

"People don't behave like that"

Untruthful defendants will usually accept the outline of the prosecution evidence, but dispute some incriminating details.

Technique: Use probing questions to explore the defendant's account, then put to her/him the more natural way of behaving. Probing questions ("Who?", "Where?", "When?", "Which?", "Why?" and "How?") can be asked very rapidly. They are easy to formulate as they merely demand more detail. The defendant will either resort to a series of "I can't remember"'s or it will become obvious s/he is making her/his evidence up as s/he goes along.

Then ask her/him very simply: "Why did you not..." and put to her/him the most natural way of acting in that situation.

"Too many coincidences"

Because untruthful defendants usually accept the outline of the prosecution evidence, but make up accounts to replace the details which they do not accept, or to account for their own behaviour, their evidence, when considered as a whole, will often contain several coincidences.

In the Crown Court, these coincidences are best left for your closing speech. In the magistrates' court the only opportunity to comment on them is in cross-examination. Put the coincidences to the defendant so s/he has the opportunity to comment on them.

Example:

The prosecution case is that the defendant stole, by taking two carrier bags of sale goods from a department store.

The defence case is that he had brought his own goods in two of the store's carrier bags, into the store, some to exchange and others to take to a dry-cleaner's.

Q. The two carrier bags you say you had brought into the store were the same sizes as the two you took out?

A. Yes, I wouldn't have made the mistake, otherwise.

Q. And it was purely co-incidental that each bag was about the same weight as the two you had brought, was it?

A. Yes.

Q. The two carrier bags you claim to have brought into the store have never been returned to you?

A. That's right.

Q. So somebody must have kept them, that is, stolen them?

A. I suppose so.

Q. It's a coincidence that someone stole your bags at about the time you mistakenly (you say) took the store's bags?

A. Yes.

Q. It's just a coincidence you did not see any goods to exchange, is it?

A. Yes.

Q. The truth is that you did not bring any bag into the store, did you?

A. Yes I did.

Q. You saw two unattended carrier bags and helped yourself to them, didn't you?

A. No.

Q. And your evidence—that you brought into the store two bags of the same size and same weight which you just happened mistakenly to take for your own bags, which have never been seen since, which were full of goods you just happened not to exchange—is all made up, isn't it?

A. No, it's the truth.

It is important to lay a foundation for this series of questions when you question the defendant about the details of his evidence.

Example:

Q. Didn't you notice a difference in weight when you picked the bags up?

A. No.

Q. They were the same weight?
A. Yes.

Driving a wedge

If it is apparent from the prosecution or defendant's evidence that one of the defendant's friends was present at the alleged offence, it is likely s/he will give evidence. You are entitled to ask the defendant whether her/his friend has attended court, but you must not ask whether the friend will give evidence (that is a matter for her/his advocate). Prepare to drive a wedge between her/his account and the defendant's. Probe the defendant's evidence.

Example I:
The defendant says he and his friend had decided to go to a bowling alley.
Ask:
When had they made that decision?
Had they been to the bowling alley before?
How often?
How recently?

Example II:
The defendant says the Victim began to behave aggressively and hit the defendant.
Ask:
What had led to the Victim's aggressive behaviour?
What did the defendant or her friend do to calm the Victim down?
How did the Victim hit the defendant?

When the friend gives her/his evidence, put the same questions. If her/his answers differ from the defendant's, put the defendant's answers to her/him.

Example:
Q. At the time the Victim was saying this, how far away were you?
A. I was only about one and a half metres in front of her.
Q. You could see everything she was doing and hear everything she said?
A. Yes.
Q. She did not gesture at the defendant?
A. No.
Q. She did not say anything about the defendant's mother?
A. No.

Finally, put to the witness the prosecution version.

Contrasting true and false answers

The defendant's answers to detailed questions are likely to differ according to whether s/he is dealing with things that really happened, or things s/he is inventing.

Technique: Lay a foundation by asking the defendant how well s/he remembers the events. Probe those answers you believe are truthful (When? Where? Why? What colour? How?, etc.). Also probe answers you believe are lies. The defendant may give the truthful answers quite quickly and confidently; then when the topic changes to details about which s/he has lied, s/he may hesitate before each answer, or take refuge in "I don't know"s. Put this difference to the defendant.

Example:

Q. Everyone accepts you went to the "Jolly Waggoner" on the Tuesday. You said you drank about three pints of lager. The assistant manager served behind the bar and so did two barmaids, one blonde-haired and one brunette. The assistant manager and the blonde barmaid had each served you at least once. The pub had been quiet. You had spoken to John Jackson and Jack Johnson. That is right, isn't it?

A. Yes.

Q. But when I asked you about going there on the Friday, you answered very differently. You were not sure what you had drunk, but you finally said no more than two pints. You couldn't remember definitely anyone who was serving behind the bar, but there was "at least one woman". You could not remember if it was she who had served you. You thought it was maybe not one of the regular staff. You thought the pub had "the usual amount of custom for a Friday night". You accepted you know a lot of the regulars in the "Waggoner" but you could not remember anyone that you were sure was there that evening. That's right, isn't it?

A. Yes.

Q. You remember the visit on Tuesday quite clearly, don't you?

A. Yes.

Q. The reason you are so unsure about the Friday visit, is that it never happened did it?

A. Yes it did.

Q. You have entirely made that account up, haven't you?

A. Not at all.

Another difference which may be apparent, is the defendant may be very precise about details of the evidence which suit her/him, and quite vague about other details. It can be put to her/him that this is because the favourable details have been invented.

"Actions speak louder than words"

Often the pattern of the undisputed evidence, including the forensic evidence, suggests the defendant's guilt and the only evidence in her/his favour is her/his own version of the disputed evidence and her/his own account of her/his motives.

Technique: Get the defendant to accept each part of the prosecution evidence, and then put to her/him the prosecution case.

Example:

Q. You accept you asked the Victim the time as he passed you on the platform?

A. Yes.

Q. You and your friends got into the carriage he was in?

A. Why shouldn't we?

Q. There were only about four other people in the carriage?

A. So what?

Q. You and your friends sat opposite to him?

A. Why shouldn't we?

Q. Then when the train had started moving you got up and sat down next to the Victim?

A. I'm entitled to sit where I like.

Q. You sat next to him to rob him?

A. That's a lie.

Q. You had asked him the time, to check him out and you thought he was a soft touch?

A. No.

Cross-Examination on Record

As a rule of thumb in your first months, do not apply to cross-examine on the defendant's record unless you are sure it is appropriate to do so. Dragging up previous convictions tends to give the impression of a case which cannot succeed on its merits and, in any case, the magistrates will have inferred from the defendant's own silence on the subject that s/he is not of good character. It is also unwise to make such an application without being familiar with authorities such as *Britzman* [1983] 1 WLR 350.

You are not entitled to cross-examine on record without leave. In the Crown Court a time-honoured formula for requesting the absence of the jury is: "May it please your Honour, a matter of law arises."

Before lay magistrates you can make an application in this way:

Example:
"May it please you, ma'am, I seek the leave of the court to cross-examine the defendant as to his character. As you are aware, s. 1 (f) (ii) of the Criminal Evidence Act of 1898 provides . . . In my submission the substance, if not the form, of his defence has involved imputations . . ."

Alternatively, you can use a formula such as:

Example:
"Sir, a matter has occurred to me on which I should like the assistance of your learned clerk. As it may take some few moments, I wonder whether you might find it more convenient to rise?"

In the absence of the bench you and the defence advocate can give your reasons why the defendant's previous convictions should, or should not, go in. If the clerk indicates s/he would advise the bench against admitting the convictions, the bench should be brought back into court and nothing more should be heard about the application. If the clerk indicates s/he would advise the bench to admit the convictions, ask the defence advocate whether s/he will consent to their admission or seek a ruling from the bench. When the bench returns, outline your application and either argue it or indicate that the defence do not object to it.

Before a stipendiary magistrate use the formula, "I have an application under the Criminal Evidence Act, 1898." S/he will tell you immediately whether s/he thinks such an application appropriate.

Cross-Examination of Defence Witnesses

Witnesses present at the alleged offence
It will usually be part of the prosecution case that the witness is lying to help a friend. Apply the same approach as to the cross-examination of the defendant. Why is the prosecution version to be preferred to the defence version? Cross-examine along the lines of that argument. Begin with the least disputed topics. Use the techniques for discrediting the evidence.

Witnesses not present at the alleged offence
A defence witness may not have been present at any alleged offence, but may corroborate material parts of the defendant's evidence.

Example I:
When stopped by the police the defendant is in possession of a video recorder.
The witness gives evidence of having been with the defendant when he bought the video recorder at a car boot sale.

Example II:
The defendant has been picked out on an ID parade as having committed a burglary.
The witness gives evidence of having been drinking in a pub with the defendant at the time of the burglary.

If the witness claims to have been present with the defendant (as in Examples I and II) the best technique is usually to probe the evidence of both, and attempt to drive a wedge between them.

If the witness was not in the defendant's company, but gives other evidence in support of the defence, consider the evidence quite neutrally. Is it a necessary part of the prosecution's case that the witness is lying, or even that s/he is wrong? Do not unnecessarily accuse a witness of lying. Your approach to each witness should be as pleasant as possible given the nature of the questions you need to ask. If the witness's evidence does not need to be challenged, the contrast between your acceptance of the witness's evidence and your scepticism about the defendant's, will help the prosecution case.

If none of the witness's evidence is challenged and you do not think you will be able to elicit from the witness anything which will assist the prosecution case, remain seated and say, "No questions". This can be the most powerful signal to the court that the witness's evidence does not damage the prosecution case.

Applications Following Conviction

While the magistrates are deliberating their verdict, consider the "four C's".

Compensation

If the offence caused damage or injury it will usually be appropriate to seek compensation for the loser/victim. In damage cases there should be a completed claim form giving details of the damage and the cost of repair or replacement and attaching estimates/invoices. Alternatively, the damage may have been quantified in the evidence (example: "It cost me £70 to repair").

If the damage has not been quantified, a claim should be made and a figure obtained for the sentencing hearing. If the court sentences immediately then it is too late to seek compensation.

Compensation can be awarded for accidental damage to a motor car in only two situations. If the defendant had taken the vehicle without the owner's permission s/he can be ordered to pay the full cost of making good the damage. Alternatively, if the damage is not covered by the defendant's insurance (if any) s/he can be ordered to pay that part of the cost of repair which is not payable by the Motor Insurers' Bureau (currently £170) (see Powers of Criminal Courts Act 1973, s.35).

A written claim form is unnecesssary for compensation for injury.

Confiscation
If the offence involved drugs or weapons seek a destruction or forfeiture order.

Previous convictions
Hand the defendant's representative a list of her/his previous convictions and ask if they are agreed. If there is a dispute, read out to the court only those which are accepted and indicate that the prosecution allege there are other, un-agreed, convictions which will have to be verified before the sentencing hearing (and endorse the file accordingly).

If any of the charges results in a conviction, immediately after the verdict has been announced, make your applications:

Example:
"The defendant does have previous convictions. I hand up a list which is agreed.

"I would ask you, ma'am, to consider making a compensation order to the owner of the car. I hand up a claim form with an invoice in the sum of £140.46.

"I would ask you, ma'am to consider making a compensation order to the Victim, and to order destruction of the machete.

"Finally, ma'am, I would ask you to consider ordering a contribution to prosecution costs. The matter was fully prepared for trial, and the amount sought is £120.

"Unless I can assist you further, ma'am, those are my applications."

Closing Speech (Crown Court only)

In the Crown Court the prosecution advocate has the right to make a closing speech unless the defendant (or all the defendants) are both unrepresented and call no evidence (other than character witnesses).

In practice the rule is: make a closing speech only if the defendant either gives or calls evidence (other than character witnesses). (See *R. v. Bryant and Oxley* [1979] Q.B. 108 on both law and practice.)

The prosecution closing speech was formerly referred to as "summing up the prosecution's evidence" which is a better description of what you should try to achieve.

A Working Plan for a Prosecution Closing Speech

(1) *Refer back to your opening speech and submit that the evidence the jury has heard does prove the defendant's guilt on each of the counts, beyond reasonable doubt, for [number] reasons, firstly...; secondly...; etc.*

(2) *Outline the first argument, making reference to the evidence as necessary*

(3) *The second argument...*

(4) *The third argument..., etc.*

(5) *Submit that for those reasons, firstly...; secondly...; etc., the proper verdict on each count is one of Guilty*

Example:

"With Your Honour's leave,

"Ladies and Gentlemen: You will remember that when I addressed you at the beginning of this case, yesterday afternoon, I said that this case has been brought by the Crown and it was for me, on behalf of the prosecution, to satisfy you that the defendants are guilty of these charges against them: it is not for the defendants to prove anything. And the standard of proof is a high one: you must be satisfied beyond reasonable doubt for it to be your duty to convict.

"The evidence you have heard does, in my submission, demonstrate beyond any reasonable doubt that both defendants are guilty.

"Each defendant faces two charges—burglary and handling—and you will remember I said they are alternatives.

"It is right that you consider the evidence against each defendant separately. The prosecution case is that this was a joint enterprise: that both defendants were working together to carry out the burglary. So I shall sum up the evidence to you without distinguishing between the defendants except for the defendant Mr Slater's interview. What he said in that interview is evidence only with regard to him. It does not affect the case of the defendant Mr Jones one way or the other.

"The reasons why this burglary must have been committed by these defendants are, firstly, the circumstances in which they were found; secondly, the fact that goods from the burglary were in their possession very soon after the burglary; thirdly, the footprint evidence; and fourthly, the prosecution say the accounts given by the defendants as to why they were in Sycamore Grove actually strengthen the prosecution case.

"Dealing, firstly, with the circumstances of the defendants' arrest. You heard evidence from PC Sharpe that...

"The second point on which the prosecution rely...

"And, fourthly, the defendants' evidence. The prosecution case, of course, is that all of that evidence is lies designed to explain away why the defendants, at four o'clock in the morning, should be in a quiet residential street somewhat over a mile away from their homes.

"Mr Slater, you will remember, claimed that they had been returning from a party. He could not name anyone at the party, not even the host, and he did not know the address where the party was held. He said they had been invited by 'a woman in a pub' in the Burnden area, though he could not say which pub...

"As I indicated earlier, ladies and gentlemen, I would ask that you first consider the burglary counts against both defendants. If you find those counts made out, it is unnecessary to consider the handling counts.

"If you find the burglary counts not proved, I would ask you then to consider the handling.

"In my submission, ladies and gentleman, the evidence you have heard can lead only to the conclusion that this burglary was committed by these defendants together, for these reasons: the defendants had goods from the burglary in their possession very shortly after the burglary; they were very nervous when stopped by the police; the footprint evidence; and finally the evidence given by the defendants contradicts each other and is, the prosecution say, so implausible as to be unbelievable.

"It therefore follows, in my submission, ladies and gentlemen, that the charges are made out, and the proper verdict against each defendant is Guilty."

Except in a long or complex case, the prosecution closing speech should always be very short.

Always address the jury argumentatively. Give the reasons why the proper verdict is Guilty, and support the reasons with reference to the evidence. Do not "remind" the jury extensively of the evidence. Only quote the actual words if it is necessary, and do so as little as possible.

Only indicate in an overall way the prosecution position on the evidence (example: that the defendant is lying); never tell the jury in detail what is believable and what is not. Do not comment favourably on the manner in which prosecution witnesses gave their evidence. And always address the jury on the (correct) assumption that they are reluctant to convict.

Example:
"If you find the defendant did so dishonestly, it will be your duty to convict."
Not:
"Only if you find the defendant did so dishonestly, will you be entitled to convict."

CHAPTER 4

REMANDS

WHENEVER YOU DO A REMAND, CONSIDER THREE THINGS:

—the legal aid position
—the bail position
—the stage the case has reached

When you arrive at court you will need information from the legal aid office/court clerk and the prosecution. Aim to see the prosecutor as soon as possible, even before seeing your client, because you may not get another chance before s/he is called into court. Be organised about the information you need from her/him because s/he will have a whole queue of advocates to deal with.

On each case you need to know:

—the charges
—the brief facts of each charge
—whether the prosecution want summary or jury trial
—your client's list of previous convictions ("form MG16")
—whether the prosecution object to unconditional bail and, if so, on what ground(s)
—whether the prosecution object to bail on conditions and, if not, what conditions are sought

If the court is already sitting when you arrive, ask the usher to keep your case back in the list, and ask her/him when the bench are likely to retire. Sit near the prosecutor and as soon as the bench go out, ask her/him about your case. If it is a stipendiary magistrate (who will not retire) write clearly on a slip of paper:

"Case of *Bloggins:*
"May I see brief facts?
"May I have copy of MG16?"

and pass this to the prosecutor. You should be able to manage with the information thus elicited.

THE LEGAL AID POSITION

After seeing the prosecutor, introduce yourself to your client, but explain to her/him that you need to check the legal aid position. Ask the legal aid officer the date from which legal aid was granted, and the legal aid number. If legal aid has not been granted, ask whether an application has been made and, if so, when it will be decided.

If not, get a legal aid form. Ask the legal aid office how soon your client needs to produce proof of income. Impress upon your client the necessity of bringing in proof of her/his means by the required date. In filling in the "reasons why legal aid should be granted" section, be realistic about why your client needs to be represented, *e.g.* "because the case will turn on the credibility of the defendant and police evidence, it is necessary the client is legally represented".

THE BAIL POSITION

Client on Bail

If your client is on bail (that is, s/he has been released from the police station after charge; or had been brought in custody to a previous court hearing at which s/he was granted bail) it may be conditional or unconditional. If it is unconditional (no conditions except to surrender to the court by turning up at the appointed time), check with your client that s/he has always attended court punctually.

If bail is conditional, check whether any of the conditions is likely to cause difficulties to the client before the next hearing *e.g.* if there is a condition of residence at her/his home address and s/he wishes to spend a weekend away from home; or if s/he has to "sign on" at ("report" to) a police station every evening between 6 and 8 p.m. and s/he has a new job which involves evening work.

If there is a problem, make an application to vary your client's bail conditions. Consider the purpose of the condition and offer alternative proposals to fulfil the same purpose (*e.g.* signing on in the morning instead of the evening). Present your application in this way:

Example:
"On [date] your colleagues granted the defendant bail on two conditions, residence at [address] and reporting to [name] police station [number] times per week. The purpose of both conditions was to ensure the defendant's attendance at court.

"My application is to vary the time of reporting to [new time]

"The reason for the application is ... [whatever]

"The new proposal is ... [whatever]

"In my submission these proposed varied conditions would ensure the defendant will attend court as directed, and I ask the court to vary her bail as outlined."

Client in Custody

If your client is in custody, you will usually want to make a bail application, but there are two circumstances in which s/he may instruct you not to.

If s/he intends to plead Guilty and expects a custodial sentence, your client may prefer to do as large a proportion as possible of that sentence on remand.

Secondly, if s/he is in custody on other matters, it would be wiser to remain in custody on these matters to ensure the time spent on remand is deducted from the eventual sentence.

THE STAGE OF THE CASE

Summary and Either-Way Offences

Road traffic

Dangerous driving is either-way. All other road traffic offences, including drunken driving, are summary. (Taking a conveyance is dealt with below.)

Dishonesty

These offences are generally either-way.

The most common summary offences are: being found on enclosed premises (Vagrancy Act 1824, s.4); motor vehicle interference; taking a conveyance without the owner's consent (aggravated TWOC is either-way); taking or riding a pedal cycle without the owner's consent. There are also some bye-law offences such as travelling on public transport without a valid ticket.

The following are all either-way: theft generally, however small the value; handling stolen goods; going equipped to steal, cheat, etc; abstracting electricity; fraudulent use of a telecommunications system.

Deception and forgery

All deception offences, including making off without payment, are either-way, except offences under the Social Security Acts, all of which are summary only.

All forgery offences are either-way, except the forgery of a vehicle excise licence (tax disc) contrary to section 26 Vehicles (Excise) Act 1971.

Violence
These offences are nearly all either-way: the only exceptions being common assault contrary to Criminal Justice Act 1988, s.39; and assault on a constable in the execution of his duty.

Weapons
The only possession offences which are summary are having a bladed instrument in a public place (Criminal Justice Act 1988, s.139(1)), and possession of a crossbow (Crossbows Act 1987, s.3).

Public order
Offences under sections 4 and 5 of the Public Order Act 1986 are summary; sections 2 and 3 are either-way.

Drugs
All possession offences are either-way.

Criminal damage
The defendant to a criminal damage charge is entitled to advance information, and mode of trial proceedings will be held. Arson offences are always either-way. In other cases, the first consideration is the value of the damage. If it is "clear" that the value does not exceed £5,000, the offence has to be tried summarily. Otherwise it remains an either-way offence.

PROCEDURE AT THE HEARING

Follow the flow diagram (page 116) to the appropriate box. The Outline (1–12 below) sets out the court procedure. The final part of each hearing is the review of the bail position, the procedure for which is as follows:

Review of Bail Position

Defendant on bail
Clerk: The defendant has been on bail on [two] conditions: [a condition of residence] and [a surety in the sum of five hundred pounds].

Defence: I ask you to continue bail on those conditions, ma'am
or:
Application to vary bail conditions (see pages 113 to 114).

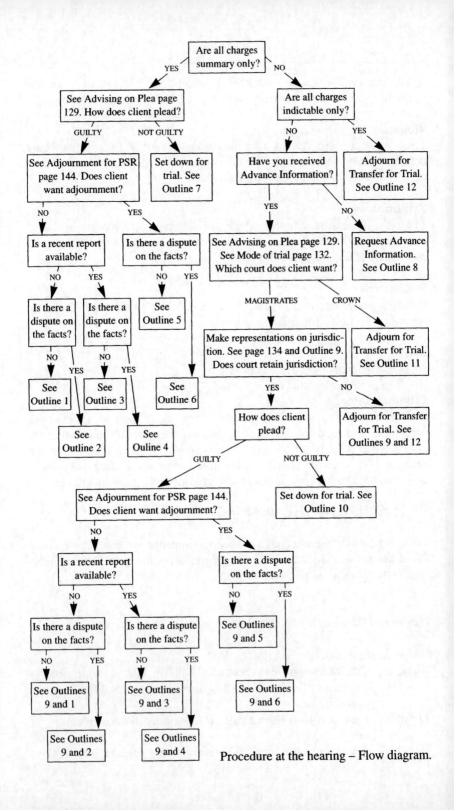

Procedure at the hearing – Flow diagram.

Bench outline conditions of bail and date of next hearing to defendant.
Defence: I'm grateful, sir / So be it, ma'am, I'm grateful.

Note: If in doubt, check Legal Aid has been granted and, if not, apply.

Defendant in custody
Clerk: Is there a bail application?
Defence: May it please you, yes.
Prosecutor outlines objections to bail.
Defence makes bail application (see page 135).
Bench withdraw.

Bench return and outline bail conditions to defendant, or give reasons for refusing bail, and confirm date of next hearing.
Defence: I'm grateful, ma'am / So be it, sir, I'm grateful.

Note: If in doubt, check Legal Aid has been granted and, if not, apply.

Outline 1

Outside court
Check with your client that s/he accepts the accuracy of the Previous Convictions (form MG16). If not, and the previous convictions may be relevant to the sentence for this matter, the case may have to be adjourned so that the defendant's record can be agreed.

Ask your client at how much per week/fortnight s/he could pay off a fine.

Prepare a bail application (see page 135), if relevant.

Inside court
Clerk identifies defendant(s).
Clerk: Can the charges be put?
Defence: Yes.
Clerk—puts charge(s) to defendant who pleads Guilty and sits down.
Prosecutor—outlines facts. Hands up Previous Convictions (form MG16)
Defence (half rises): It's agreed.
Prosecutor—applies for compensation/forfeiture/destruction orders as
　　　　　　appropriate. Applies for costs.
Defence: Seeks to persuade court to sentence defendant without
　　　　　　obtaining a pre-sentence report (a fine or a conditional/
　　　　　　absolute discharge is the only likely disposal).
　　　　　　See Working Plan on page 148, adapted on page 155.
Bench withdraws—then either of below.

Immediate sentence	Pre-sentence report ordered
Bench returns and passes sentence.	Bench returns.
Defence: I wonder if you would allow the defendant to pay the compensation/fine/costs at the rate of £x per week/fortnight. That would mean the whole amount would be paid off in y weeks.	Bench: No, there must be a report.
	Clerk sets date for sentencing hearing.
	Proceed to Review of Bail Position (see page 115).
Bench: Yes / No, it must be £z per week/fortnight.	
Defence: I'm most grateful, ma'am / So be it, sir, I'm most grateful.	

Outline 2

Outside court

Check with your client that s/he accepts the accuracy of the Previous Convictions (form MG16). If not, and the previous convictions may be relevant to the sentence for this matter, the case may have to be adjourned so that the defendant's record can be agreed.

Ask your client at how much per week/fortnight s/he could pay off a fine.

Prepare a bail application (see page 135), if relevant.

Inside court

Clerk identifies defendant(s).

Clerk: Can the charges be put?

Defence: Yes.

Clerk—puts charge(s) to defendant who pleads Guilty and sits down.

Prosecutor—indicates that the facts are in dispute. Opens prosecution version of facts. Hands up Previous Convictions (form MG16).

Defence (half rises): It's agreed.

Prosecutor—applies for compensation/forfeiture/destruction orders as appropriate. Applies for costs.

Defence: May it please you, sir; as my friend indicates, some of the facts are in dispute.
[Outlines defendant's version of facts.]

In my submission, these areas of disagreement are not so significant as to affect sentence, and therefore it is not necessary to go to the trouble and expense of calling evidence.

Bench considers.

Newton hearing

Bench: The two versions of the facts differ so widely that sentence would be affected.

Clerk: Then there will have to be a Newton hearing. How many witnesses will the parties call? What is the time estimate? Are there any dates to avoid?

Clerk sets date for Newton hearing.

Proceed to Review of Bail Position (see page 115).

No Newton hearing

Bench: The difference between the two versions of the facts would not affect sentence.

Defence: I'm grateful, sir. I seek to persuade you that it is unnecessary to obtain a pre-sentence report before sentencing the defendant. [A fine or a conditional/absolute discharge is the only likely disposal.]

(See Working Plan on page 148, adapted on page 155.)

Bench withdraws—then either of below.

Immediate sentence

Bench returns and passes sentence.

Defence: I wonder if you would allow the defendant to pay the compensation/fine/costs at the rate of $£x$ per week/fortnight. That would mean the whole amount would be paid off in y weeks.

Bench: Yes / No, it must be $£z$ per week/fortnight.

Defence: I'm most grateful, ma'am / So be it, sir, I'm most grateful.

Pre-sentence report ordered

Bench returns.

Bench: No, there must be a report.

Clerk sets date for sentencing hearing.

Proceed to Review of Bail Position (see page 115).

Outline 3

Outside court

Check with your client that s/he accepts the accuracy of the Previous Convictions (form MG16). If not, and the previous convictions may be relevant to the sentence for this matter, the case may have to be adjourned so that the defendant's record can be agreed.

Ask your client at how much per week/fortnight s/he could pay off a fine.

Prepare a bail application (see page 135), if relevant.

Inside court

Clerk identifies defendant(s).

Clerk: Can the charges be put?

Defence: Yes.

Clerk   —puts charge(s) to defendant who pleads Guilty and sits down.

Prosecutor—outlines facts. Hands up Previous Convictions (form MG16)

Defence (half rises): It's agreed.

Prosecutor—applies for compensation/forfeiture/destruction orders as appropriate. Applies for costs.

Defence: —May it please you, ma'am; I ask you to sentence the defendant on the basis of a report prepared for the [name of] court for a hearing on [date]. Copies are available. The defendant tells me there has been [only one] significant change in his circumstances since the report was prepared, and I am fully instructed on it. In these circumstances, ma'am, I submit it is unnecessary to order a further report.

Bench considers—then either of below.

New report ordered	Sentence on recent report
Bench: No, there must be an up-to-date report.	Bench: Yes, we will sentence on the basis of the report that is available.
Clerk sets date for sentencing hearing.	Defence: I'm grateful, ma'am.
	Plea in mitigation (see Working Plan, page 148).
Proceed to Review of Bail Position (see page 115).	Bench withdraws.
	Bench passes sentence.
	Defence: I wonder if you would allow the defendant to pay the compensation/fine/costs at the

rate of £x per week/fortnight. That would mean the whole amount would be paid off in y weeks.

Bench: Yes / No, it must be £z per week/fortnight.

Defence: I'm most grateful, ma'am / So be it, sir, I'm most grateful.

Outline 4

Outside court

Check with your client that s/he accepts the accuracy of the Previous Convictions (form MG16). If not, and the previous convictions may be relevant to the sentence for this matter, the case may have to be adjourned so that the defendant's record can be agreed.

Ask your client at how much per week/fortnight s/he could pay off a fine.

Prepare a bail application (see page 135), if relevant.

Inside court

Clerk identifies defendant(s).

Clerk: Can the charges be put?

Defence: Yes.

Clerk —puts charge(s) to defendant who pleads Guilty and sits down.

Prosecutor—indicates that the facts are in dispute. Opens prosecution version of facts. Hands up Previous Convictions (form MG16)

Defence (half rises): It's agreed.

Prosecutor—applies for compensation/forfeiture/destruction orders as appropriate. Applies for costs.

Defence: May it please you, sir; as my friend indicates, some of the facts are in dispute. [Outlines defendant's version of facts.] In my submission, these areas of disagreement are not so significant as to affect sentence, and therefore it is not necessary to go to the trouble and expense of calling evidence.

Bench considers.

Newton hearing

Bench: The two versions of the facts differ so widely that sentence would be affected.

Clerk: Then there will have to be a Newton hearing. How many witnesses will the parties call? What is the time estimate? Are there any dates to avoid?

Clerk sets date for Newton hearing.

Proceed to Review of Bail Position (see page 115 above).

No Newton hearing

Bench: The difference between the two versions of the facts would not affect sentence.

Defence: I'm grateful, sir. I ask you to sentence the defendant on the basis of a report prepared for the [name of] court for a hearing on [date]. Copies are available. The defendant tells me there has been [only one] significant change in his circumstances since the report was prepared, and I am fully instructed on it. In these circumstances, sir, I submit it is unnecessary to order a further report.

Bench considers—then either.

#### New report ordered	#### Sentence on recent report
Bench: No, there must be an up-to-date report.	Bench: Yes, we will sentence on the basis of the report that is available.
Clerk sets date for sentencing hearing.	Defence: I'm grateful, ma'am.
	Plea in mitigation (see Working Plan, page 148).
Proceed to Review of Bail Position (see page 115).	Bench withdraws.
	Bench passes sentence.
	Defence: I wonder if you would allow the defendant to pay the compensation/fine/costs at the rate of £x per week/fortnight. That would mean the whole amount would be paid off in y weeks.
	Bench: Yes / No, it must be £z per week/fortnight.
	Defence: I'm most grateful, ma'am / So be it, sir, I'm most grateful.

Outline 5

Outside court
Check with your client that s/he accepts the accuracy of the Previous Convictions (form MG16). If not, and the previous convictions may be relevant to the sentence for this matter, the case may have to be adjourned so that the defendant's record can be agreed.

Ask your client at how much per week/fortnight s/he could pay off a fine.

Prepare a bail application (see page 135), if relevant.

Inside court
Clerk identifies defendant(s).

Clerk: Can the charges be put?

Defence: Yes.

Clerk— puts charge(s) to defendant who pleads Guilty and sits down.

Prosecutor—outlines facts. Hands up Previous Convictions (form MG16)

Defence (half rises): It's agreed.

Prosecutor—applies for compensation/forfeiture/destruction orders as appropriate. Applies for costs.

Defence: I imagine, sir, you would want a report?

Bench: Yes.

Clerk sets date for sentencing hearing.

Proceed to Review of Bail Position (see page 115).

Outline 6

Outside court
Check with your client that s/he accepts the accuracy of the Previous Convictions (form MG16). If not, and the previous convictions may be relevant to the sentence for this matter, the case may have to be adjourned so that the defendant's record can be agreed.

Ask your client at how much per week/fortnight s/he could pay off a fine.

Prepare a bail application (see page 135), if relevant.

Inside court
Clerk identifies defendant(s).

Clerk: Can the charges be put?

Defence: Yes.

Clerk— puts charge(s) to defendant who pleads Guilty and sits down.

Prosecutor—indicates that the facts are in dispute. Opens prosecution version of facts. Hands up Previous Convictions (form MG16)

Defence (half rises): It's agreed.

Prosecutor—applies for compensation/forfeiture/destruction orders as appropriate. Applies for costs.

Defence: May it please you, sir; as my friend indicates, some of the facts are in dispute. [Outlines defendant's version of facts.] In my submission, these areas of disagreement are not so significant as to affect sentence, and therefore it is not necessary to go to the trouble and expense of calling evidence.

Bench considers.

Newton hearing

Bench: The two versions of the facts differ so widely that sentence would be affected.

Clerk: Then there will have to be a Newton hearing. How many witnesses will the parties call? What is the time estimate? Are there any dates to avoid?

Clerk sets date for Newton hearing.

Proceed to Review of Bail Position (see page 115).

No Newton hearing

Bench: The difference between the two versions of the facts would not affect sentence.

Defence: I'm grateful, ma'am. I imagine you would require a report?

Bench: Yes.

Clerk sets date for sentencing hearing.

Proceed to Review of Bail Position (see page 115).

Outline 7

Outside court

Prepare a bail application (see page 135), if relevant.

Inside court

Clerk identifies defendant(s).

Clerk: Can the charges be put?

Defence: Yes.

Clerk— puts charge(s) to defendant who pleads Not Guilty and sits down.

Prosecutor: Three prosecution witnesses, dates to avoid are [dates].

Defence: Only the defendant. I would estimate one and a half to two hours. Dates to avoid are [dates].
Clerk sets date for trial.
Proceed to Review of Bail Position (see page 115).

Outline 8

Outside court
Prepare a bail application (see page 135), if relevant.

Inside court
Clerk identifies defendant(s) and outlines charges(s).
Clerk: What is the application? / Can we proceed to mode of trial?
Defence: My application is for Advance Information.
Prosecutor: I request two weeks to prepare the Advance Information.
Clerk sets date for service of Advance Information.
Proceed to Review of Bail Position (see page 115).

Outline 9

Outside court
Check with your client that s/he accepts the accuracy of the Previous Convictions (form MG16). If not, and the previous convictions may be relevant to the sentence for this matter, the case may have to be adjourned so that the defendant's record can be agreed.

Ask your client at how much per week/fortnight s/he could pay off a fine.

Prepare a bail application (see page 135), if relevant.

Inside court
Clerk identifies defendant(s) and outlines charge(s).
Clerk: What is the application? / Can we proceed to mode of trial?
Defence: Yes, ma'am.

Prosecution say suitable
Prosecutor: The prosecution say this case is suitable for summary trial. (Outlines facts and reasons why suitable.)
Defence: May it please you, ma'am; in my submission this case is well within your jurisdiction and I agree with everything my friend has said. I do not wish to take up court time unnecessarily, but if there were any question of your declining jurisdiction, I would wish to make representations.

(If court retains jurisdiction, proceed as at "Bench retain jurisdiction" below.)

(If court wishes to be addressed on suitability for summary trial, proceed as at "Prosecution say unsuitable" below.)

Prosecution say unsuitable

Prosecutor: The prosecution say this case is not suitable for summary trial. (Outlines facts and reasons why not suitable.)

Defence: Ma'am, I seek to persuade you that it would be right for the court to retain jurisdiction, for these reasons...

Makes representation that case is suitable for summary trial (see Working Plan for Mode of Trial Representations, page 134).

Bench consider.

Bench decline jurisdiction

Proceed as at Outline 12.

Bench retain jurisdiction

Bench: We find the case suitable for summary trial.

Clerk: Can the charges be put?

Defence: Yes.

Clerk— puts charge(s) to defendant who pleads Guilty, and sits down.

Prosecutor—outlines facts. Hands up Previous Convictions (form MG16)

Defence (half rises): It's agreed.

Prosecutor—applies for compensation/forfeiture/destruction orders as appropriate. Applies for costs.

Facts not in dispute	Facts in dispute
If defendant wants a report to be prepared, proceed as at Outline 5.	If defendant wants a report to be prepared, proceed as at Outline 6.
If defendant wants to be sentenced on the basis of a recent report, proceed as at Outline 3.	If defendant wants to be sentenced on the basis of a recent report, proceed as at Outline 4.
If there is no report and defendant wants to be sentenced without an adjournment for one, proceed as at Outline 1.	If there is no report and defendant wants to be sentenced without an adjournment for one, proceed as at Outline 2.

Outline 10

Outside court
Prepare a bail application (see page 135), if relevant.

Inside court
Clerk identifies defendant(s) and outlines charge(s).

Clerk: What is the application? / Can we proceed to mode of trial?

Defence: Yes, ma'am.

Prosecution say suitable
Prosecutor: The prosecution say this case is suitable for summary trial. (Outlines facts and reasons why suitable.)

Defence: May it please you, ma'am; in my submission this case is well within your jurisdiction and I agree with everything my friend has said. I do not wish to take up court time unnecessarily, but if there were any question of your declining jurisdiction, I would wish to make representations.

(If court retains jurisdiction, proceed as at "Bench retain jurisdiction" below.)

(If court wishes to be addressed on suitability for summary trial, proceed as at "Prosecution say unsuitable" below.)

Prosecution say unsuitable
Prosecutor: The prosecution say this case is not suitable for summary trial. (Outlines facts and reasons why not suitable.)

Defence: Ma'am, I seek to persuade you that it would be right for the court to retain jurisdiction, for these reasons...

Makes representation that case is suitable for summary trial (see Working Plan for Mode of Trial Representations, page 134).

Bench consider—then either of below.

Bench decline jurisdiction	*Bench retain jurisdiction*
Proceed as at Outline 12.	Bench: We find the case suitable for summary trial.
	Clerk: Can the charges be put?
	Defence: Yes.
	Clerk—puts charge(s) to defendant who pleads Not Guilty and sits down.
	Prosecutor: Three prosecution witnesses, dates to avoid are [dates].

> Defence: Only the defendant. I would estimate one and a half to two hours. Dates to avoid are [dates].
> Clerk sets date for trial.
> Proceed to Review of Bail Position (see page 115).

Outline 11

Outside court
Prepare a bail application (see page 135), if relevant.

Inside court
Clerk identifies defendant(s) and outlines charge(s).

Clerk: What is the application? / Can we proceed to mode of trial?

Defence: Yes, sir.

Prosecutor: The prosecution say this case is suitable for summary trial for these reasons... / The prosecution say this case is not suitable for summary trial for these reasons...

Clerk: Have the defence any representions?

Defence (half-rising): No representations.

Clerk (to defendant): This court feels this case is more suitable for summary trial, but it is your decision whether you be tried by this court or before a judge and jury. However, I must warn you that if you plead Guilty or are found Guilty in this court and, after learning more about you, the magistrates feel their powers of punishment are insufficient, you will be committed for sentence to the Crown Court. Do you wish to be tried in this court or the Crown Court?

Defendant: Crown Court, please.

Clerk: The case will have to be adjourned for transfer for trial.

Clerk sets date for transfer.

Proceed to Review of Bail Position (see page 115).

Outline 12

Outside court
Prepare a bail application (see page 135), if relevant.

Inside court

Clerk identifies defendant(s).

Clerk: This charge is / all these charges are indictable only. A date will have to be set for transfer for trial.

Clerk sets date for transfer.

Proceed to Review of Bail Position (see page 115).

ADVISING ON PLEA

Your client must enter her/his plea her/himself (s/he must say the words "Guilty" or "Not Guilty"), and it is her/his decision which plea to enter to each charge.

Summary Offences

Ask the prosecutor to let you read the witness statements or give you full details of the allegations. If the court is already sitting and it is difficult to talk to the her/him, ask the court office for the details from the charge sheet or summons (which will be on computer). If the case is at all complex or your client is unsure of her/his plea, ask the prosecution to give voluntary advance information and seek an adjournment for it to be served and considered.

Either-way Offences

Your client may be in a position to enter her/his plea without seeing the Advance Information because s/he knows whether or not s/he is guilty. If your client wants advice on plea, there will be little you can say until you have read the Advance Information, so if there is any doubt as to plea and Advance Information is not available, request it.

A Case on Paper?

In advising on plea, first consider whether there is a case on the papers. Apply the "Four F's" filter (see pages 20–22). Is there some evidence on each element of each offence ("Full?")? If there is at least one gap in the prosecution case and the offences are summary-only, or your client is intending to consent to summary trial, it may well be worth pleading Not Guilty, because it is very possible the prosecution case will not be further reviewed, and the gap will remain.

If the case is going to the Crown Court, the evidence will be further reviewed and, almost certainly, the gap closed with Additional Evidence. If there is a gap in the prosecution evidence which you think the prosecution either may not (because the case will remain in the magistrates' court) or cannot (because the evidence may be unobtainable) fill, but your client nevertheless decides to plead Guilty, ask her/him to endorse your instructions.

Example:
"I have been advised that the witness statements do not identify me as the man who broke the window. Despite this advice I have decided to plead Guilty."

Would the admission of any of the evidence be so unfair that it ought not be to admitted ("Fair?")? If an essential part of the evidence (for example, of *mens rea*) is likely to be excluded, you will consider carefully whether to advise a plea of Not Guilty.

How is your client identified ("Fingered?")? Always scrutinise the identification evidence closely.

Before turning to the Facts, consider whether all the necessary prosecution witnesses will turn up. If any of them is known to your client, ask her/him. In the magistrates' court, if s/he thinks one necessary witness may not turn up, it is almost certainly worth pleading Not Guilty. In the Crown Court it may be worth pleading Not Guilty depending on how confident your client is that the witness will not attend.

If there is a case on paper and the witnesses are all strangers to your client, explain what is being alleged against her/him and ask how s/he intends to plead.

Facts in Dispute

If Guilty, ask whether s/he accepts the facts as stated by the prosecution. If not, take down your client's version of events, taking care not to lead.

A dispute as to the facts on a plea of Guilty can be dealt with in three ways. If there is an opportunity, speak to the prosecutor. You may be able to agree a version of the facts acceptable to both parties. Alternatively, you may be able to agree that the dispute is unlikely to have a significant effect on sentence. The prosecutor can then open the agreed facts to the sentencing court or, alternatively, indicate to the court that there is a dispute on the facts, and open the prosecution version. You will then put your client's version of the facts and, unless the court hears evidence, it is upon the basis of the defence version that the court must sentence (*Newton* (1982) 77 Cr. App. R. 13, 15).

The second possibility is that no agreement is reached between the parties. The prosecutor indicates to the court that there is a dispute as to the facts, and opens the prosecution version. You will then put your client's version of the facts and represent to the court that it is unnecessary to hear evidence. If the court accepts this, it must sentence upon the basis of the defence version of the facts.

The third possibility is that the court will decide that the disparity between the two versions would affect sentence to such an extent that evidence must be heard. The case will then be set down for a Newton hearing on the facts, and those witnesses whose evidence is disputed and relevant to the gravity of the offence will be warned to attend.

Client Intends to Plead "Not Guilty"

If your client tells you s/he intends to plead Not Guilty, ask her/him some questions about the nature of her/his defence, *e.g.* does s/he deny being at the scene?; does s/he accept being at the scene, but deny the behaviour alleged?; or admit the behaviour but claim justification? When you understand the nature of her/his defence, consider how likely it is to succeed.

Secondly, consider the likely reduction in sentence if the defendant pleaded Guilty at an early stage. There are a number of factors to take into account in estimating the size of the discount. Reductions are smaller the stronger the evidence against the defendant, and very small if s/he is caught "red-handed". There is less discount in the magistrates' court than in the Crown Court, and in the youth court almost no reduction (notwithstanding section 48 of the Criminal Justice and Public Order Act 1994). The discount is larger when the plea obviates the need for a victim to give evidence, and the more distressing the nature of the evidence avoided, the greater the discount in sentence. Even a last minute change of plea, if it saves a witness from having to give distressing evidence, will receive credit.

Often a useful opening is to ask your client how likely s/he thinks it is that s/he will be acquitted. The reply may range from "I'm sure of it", to "No chance, but it's worth a try, isn't it?".

If the defendant is realistic about her/his chances of conviction, consider the likely sentence. If in your view the plea is likely to mean the difference between a conditional discharge and a fine, or a community sentence and custody, point out to your client that should s/he be convicted after a plea of Not Guilty there is little you can say about the facts of the offence which will have been presented in all their vividness to the convicting court; but that on a plea of Guilty they would simply be read out by the prosecutor, and you would then be in a position to explain how your client had come to behave as s/he had. Sentence would be reduced by the plea of Guilty. Once you have explained this, it is a matter for your client to decide.

If you consider the reduction in sentence is unlikely to be very much, and your client is realistic about her/his chances of conviction, you can move on to discuss mode of trial or, in a summary case, preparation for trial.

If your client does not appreciate how likely s/he is to be convicted, point out to her/him that the jury/magistrates were not present at the incident and can only go by the evidence. Point out the strength of the prosecution evidence and that the jury/magistrates, who do not know the defendant, may not appreciate that her/his evidence is the truth. Where a relatively minor offence carries stigma (shoplifting, for example) your client may well find it easier to live with what s/he considers a wrongful conviction than an admission of guilt.

It is, of course, difficult to draw a line between railroading a client into an unwilling plea of Guilty on the one hand, and setting her/him along the road to certain conviction, on the other. It may help to keep in mind that the aim of your advice is to enable your client to come to her/his own decision.

If there is any doubt, enter a plea of Not Guilty and, in any eitherway case, elect jury trial.

But do stress to your client that s/he should consider her/his plea very carefully and, if s/he wishes to change it, to contact her/his solicitor very quickly, to maximise the reduction for a plea of Guilty; and, in an eitherway case, to enable an application under the Magistrates Courts Act 1980, s.6 to be made.

MODE OF TRIAL

The general rule is: fight in the Crown Court, plead in the magistrates'. The conviction rate in the Crown Court is significantly lower. In the magistrates' courts, sentences are appreciably lighter and are more easily appealed against.

There are a number of exceptions to the general rule. If you feel your client's chances of acquittal are very low, but s/he refuses to plead Guilty, you might advise her/him to consider summary trial. It is a half-way house, because s/he presumably thinks s/he has a worthwhile chance of acquittal, whereas you think s/he would serve her/himself best by pleading Guilty, thereby giving you a free rein to mitigate. If, however, your client tells you s/he is not guilty, but accepts s/he faces a high risk of conviction, summary trial may be the least unsatisfactory option.

The next three exceptions derive from the fact that cases for summary trial are, on the whole, significantly less well prepared than those tried on indictment. Sometimes there is a gap in the prosecution evidence.

Example:
Your client is found with a herbal substance in his pocket.
A scientist analyses a herbal substance and determines that it is cannabis.
There is no evidence to show the herbal substances are one and the same.

If such a case goes to the Crown Court it will be reviewed and a memorandum will be sent by the Crown Prosecution Service to the police who will prepare an additional statement closing the gap. If the case were simply set down for trial in the magistrates' court there is a chance that no further work will be done on the file and, at trial, you will be able to make a successful half-time submission.

Example:
"May it please you ma'am; my submission at this stage is that the prosecution evidence does not amount to a case to answer.
"It is not in dispute that on arrest there was, in the defendant's pocket, a herbal substance which the police seized. But there is no further evidence about that substance..."

A second, closely-related exception, is where there is a prosecution case (there is evidence on every element), but the evidence is not well-prepared. It may be that the evidence is difficult to follow because it is muddled, or the prosecution have neglected to take a statement from a witness. If the case is set for trial, it is very likely there will be no further evidence, and what evidence there is may well emerge in a muddled form.

If the case is transferred to the Crown Court Additional Evidence may be served; and because the case will have to be opened to a jury, more thought is likely to be given to the presentation of the evidence, and the appearance of muddle can be reduced by a well-worded opening. The defendant may, therefore, have a better chance in the magistrates' court.

The third exception is where you have a submission on the law which you think is borderline in its chances of being upheld. Such a submission has a better chance of success in the magistrates' court. Lay magistrates and their clerks are more open to persuasion by carefully made submissions than Crown Court judges, and may be more likely to prefer to err on the side of the defendant. Moreover, if your submission fails, you can have a second bite of the cherry on appeal to the Crown Court. Alternatively you can run the case in the magistrates' solely on legal submissions and, if those fail, call evidence in the Crown Court.

A final exception is that some clients may simply find the Crown Court too much of an ordeal, in which case it may be better, and almost certainly quicker, for them to stand trial in the magistrates' court.

However, you should certainly point out to them that the conviction rate is lower in the Crown Court and that jury trial may very possibly be no more of an ordeal than trial in the magistrates' court.

The only circumstance in which it would be wise for a defendant who intends to plead Guilty to elect Crown Court trial, is to join the offence up with others for which s/he is due to be sentenced, and so get a discount for bulk.

Nevertheless, it is extremely common for defendants to elect Crown Court trial, despite having been offered summary trial, and then plead Guilty upon arraignment. Inevitably they receive sentences heavier than they would have been given in the magistrates'. Sometimes they have been held in custody awaiting Crown Court, whereas they would have been given bail at the magistrates' on a plea of Guilty and, following reports, a community sentence. This can happen only because the defendant had not, prior to mode of trial, received advice good enough to enable her/him to decide properly on plea and, in particular, advice that sentencing in the magistrates' courts is lighter.

Representations on Jurisdiction

If your client has decided to elect jury trial, when you are asked whether you have any representations on mode of trial, simply say, "No representations" (saying anything further is a badge of inexperience).

If your client wants summary trial, you must do everything you can to ensure jurisdiction is retained. Where the prosecution have represented the case is suitable for summary trial and the allegation seems well within the jurisdiction of the magistrates' court, you will not need to address the court at length (see Outline 9, at page 125).

Where the prosecution have represented that the case is not suitable for summary trial, or the bench seem reluctant to retain jurisdiction, it is important that you make very forceful representations that summary jurisdiction is suitable.

Mode of trial representations should always be brief and closely-argued. Your manner should be one of assisting the court to make the right decision. Make sure you have a copy of the revised Mode of Trial Guidelines in front of you (they are in Blackstone's and Stone's, and the court will have copies).

A Working Plan for Mode of Trial Representations

(1) *May it please you, ma'am; in my submission this is an offence over which it would be right for this court to retain jurisdiction, for these reasons ...*

(2) *In the* Mode of Trial Guidelines *reported in the Weekly Law*

*Reports for 1990, volume 1, at page 1439, the learned Chief Justice indicated that generally either-way offences should be tried summarily unless there was both one of a list of aggravating features **and** the court's sentencing powers are insufficient*

(3a) *The possible aggravating features of offences of this type are* ...

These can be taken from the Guidelines.

Deal with the facts of the case, demonstrating the absence, or near absence, of aggravating features.

Although I, of course, accept the seriousness of this offence, this court does regularly deal with very serious matters and, in my submission, in this particular offence none of the aggravating features mentioned in the guidelines, is present

or (more likely):

(3b) *I, of course, accept that, as my friend says, one [or two] of the aggravating features mentioned in the guidelines is present in this offence. However, it is a two-limb test and* ...

Consider sentencing guidelines and likely sentence.

...in my submission, bearing in mind the court's power to commit for sentence should the individual case merit it, the court's sentencing powers are ample

(4) *Make any other points on the general guidelines, e.g. that there are neither complex questions of fact nor difficult questions of law. Mention any other circumstances which make summary trial more suitable*

(5) *For those reason, ma'am; I ask you to retain jurisdiction. Unless I can assist you further, that is my submission*

BAIL APPLICATION

Is your client entitled to apply for bail?

It is submitted that the rule is: a defendant is entitled to apply for bail once only, with two exceptions: firstly, an application made on her/his first appearance is not counted; and secondly, s/he may make a fresh application every time her/his circumstances change. This, it is submitted, is the effect of Part IIA of Schedule 1 to the Bail Act 1976.

The provisions of the Bail Act are expressed less clearly than they might be, and as practice varies between magistrates' courts, it is always worth attempting to make an application.

Prosecution objections

Ask the prosecutor for a copy of your client's Previous Convictions ("form MG16"), and ask whether s/he objects to unconditional bail.

If so, ask (i) on what grounds; (ii) on what information the objections are based (there may be outstanding warrants, for example); and (iii) whether there are conditions (and if so, which) on which the prosecution would not object to bail.

Always consider the form MG16 carefully. Apart from previous offences of Failure to Attend court, look for convictions for attempting to pervert the course of justice, evidence of drug addiction and whether, from the dates of the convictions, it is apparent that the defendant has in the past committed offences whilst on bail. It is the one document the magistrates have in front of them in a bail application, so it is necessary to have taken instructions on anything apparent from it, and essential not to misquote it.

Taking Instructions

Routine questions

Whenever you prepare a bail application, ask your client these questions:

(1)   If granted bail, at what address would s/he live?

(2)   Whose property is it?

(3)   If it is a tenancy, what sort (local authority; housing association; private?) and in whose name?

(4)   Who else lives there?

(5)   For how long have your client and the tenant (if different) lived there?

(6)   What work does your client do; where; and what hours?

(7)   Would your client be caused any difficulties by having to sleep every night at her/his address?

(8)   What difficulties would s/he be caused by having to remain indoors at home between, say, 8 p.m. and 7 a.m.?

(9)   If s/he had to report regularly to a police station what time, and what station, would be the most convenient?

(10) Would your client be caused any special problems, other than the obvious ones, by being refused bail?

Obtaining a picture

The questions you ask to get the "feel" of your client's circumstances will vary according to her/his age. Most defendants are young men. It will usually be appropriate to ask:

(1)   How long has s/he lived in the area?

(2)   When did s/he leave school?

(3) With what qualifications?
(4) What training has s/he done since then?
(5) What work (including Saturday jobs) has s/he done?
(6) What plans for work or training does s/he have?
(7) Is s/he in a relationship?
(8) Does s/he have children?

With an older client, there are likely to be more questions about her/his past. Her/his schooling is irrelevant, but it will probably be useful to know whether, predominantly, s/he has been in or out of work, and what sort of work. What ties does s/he have in the area?

Preparing the Application

All submissions in court should be made argumentatively. In a bail application your argument is either that there is no valid objection to unconditional bail; or that the objections can be met by attaching conditions to bail. The three main objections are that the defendant would:

(a) fail to surrender to custody
(b) commit further offences
(c) interfere with witnesses

Occasionally the prosecution add that the defendant should be kept in custody for his own protection (Bail Act 1976, Sched. 1, Pt. I, paras. 2 and 3). The court has regard to:

(a) the nature and seriousness of the alleged offence and the probable sentence for it
(b) the character, antecedents, associations and community ties of the defendant
(c) any previous failures to surrender
(d) the strength of the evidence against the defendant

(Bail Act 1976, Sched 1, Part I, para 9.)

Failure to Surrender

Problems

(1) Past failures to surrender, especially recent ones.
(2) The likelihood of a prison sentence.
(3) Appearing at the present hearing on a warrant, having failed to attend in these proceedings.
(4) Being unemployed.
(5) Having few community ties.
(6) Being unable to live at her/his usual address (*e.g.* because the Victim lives there or nearby).

Positive factors
(1) The failures to attend being very old.
(2) A convincing explanation of non-attendance earlier in these proceedings.
(3) Having attended court in previous proceedings when a prison sentence was likely.
(4) Being able to offer an alternative address (*e.g.* a relative's).
(5) Owning own home, or having own tenancy.
(6) Being able to obtain, and willing to accept, a place in a bail hostel.
(7) Being able to offer a surety.
(8) A convincing offer of employment. Unless it is written it may be treated with scepticism by the court but, unless you think their scepticism may extend to the rest of your submissions, there is no harm in mentioning an offer which is not in writing.

Questions
(1) Tell your client you do not want to know about any failures to surrender other than those of which you have been informed by the prosecutor and those on her/his list of previous convictions (form MG16). Ask her/him whether s/he admits those failures.
(2) If your client has been brought to court on a warrant, ask her/him why s/he did not attend court when s/he should have done, and continue to question her/him until you thoroughly understand what happened.
(3) Is there anywhere else your client could live if the court do not wish her/him to return to her/his usual address?
(4) If your client had to sleep every night at her/his bail address, would that cause her/him any problems (*e.g.* because s/he has to travel for work)?
(5) If necessary, which would be the most convenient police station to report to, and at what times?
(6) If necessary, would your client live at a bail hostel?
(7) Has your client ever attended court expecting a prison sentence?

Commission of Further Offences

Problems
(1) The present offence's having been allegedly committed whilst your client is on bail for another matter.
(2) Having committed offences in the past whilst on bail.
(3) Having an addiction which leads to offending.

Positive factors
(1) An intention to plead Not Guilty, coupled with weak evidence.
(2) Treatment of an addiction.
(3) Being able to obtain, and willing to accept, a place in a bail hostel.
(4) Bail support programme.
(5) Curfew, if offending took place at particular times of day.
(6) A restriction on entering certain areas (*e.g.* the London Underground, in the case of a pickpocket; the area where an assault victim lives).

Questions
(1) Ask your client whether s/he admits or does not admit that certain offences were committed whilst on bail (you can work out from the dates of the offences on the list of previous convictions whether any of them are likely to have been committed whilst on bail).
(2) If the present offence is said to have been committed whilst on bail for another matter, ask your client whether s/he intends to plead Guilty or Not Guilty to that matter.
(3) If the details of the allegation suggest an addiction, does your client have any definite plans to receive treatment for it?
(4) If necessary, would your client live at a bail hostel?
(5) Would your client abide by a curfew or restriction on her/his freedom of movement?

Interference with Witnesses

Problems
(1) Convictions for attempting to pervert the course of justice.
(2) Allegations of threats to witnesses.
(3) Witnesses being workmates or neighbours.
(4) Witnesses being elderly or otherwise vulnerable.

Positive factors
(1) The defendant living at an address away from the witnesses.
(2) Prohibition on entering areas where witnesses are likely to be.

Questions
(1) Does your client actually know the whereabouts of any prosecution witnesses?
(2) Is there somewhere else your client could live if the court did not wish her/him to return to her/his usual address?

(3)   Would your client abide by a prohibition on entering certain areas?

In custody for her/his own protection

If there is a significant risk the defendant may be attacked, the most effective condition of bail is likely to be that s/he live at an address outside the area.

A Working Plan for a Bail Application

(1)   *The prosecutor will begin by stating her/his objections to bail and possibly suggesting conditions on which bail may be granted*

If (on instructions) these conditions are definitely acceptable to your client, indicate to the court that you seek bail on those terms.

If the court accepts these joint submissions, it only remains for you to provide the details of the conditions (*e.g.* place of residence; name of police station; name of a surety and whether s/he is in court or will attend a police station to be taken).

(2)   *Indicate the conditions on which you are seeking bail, or that you are seeking unconditional bail (with conditions as a fall-back)*

(3)   *Remind the court the defendant has a right to bail unless there are substantial grounds for believing one of the objections is made out*

Bail Act 1976, Sched. 1, Pt. I, para. 2.

(4a)   *State that although you accept the court will be concerned about the possibility of [one objection] and [another objection], in your submission the concerns can be adequately met by conditions [1], [2] and [3]*

or

(4b)   *State that in your submission none of the prosecution objections is made out*

(5)   *Deal with each objection in turn, demonstrating either that there is not a substantial risk; or by suggesting conditions to meet the objection*

(6)   *Give some background information about your client, emphasising the unlikelihood of the objection materialising*

(7)   *State any particular consequences of a refusal of bail*

For example, a special occasion the defendant would miss.

(8)   *Summarise briefly the conditions you are asking for*

Making the Application

A successful bail application works on two levels. The prosecution's objections are met with argument to show they are ill-founded or can be met by the imposition of suitable conditions. At a less rational level, the court is made to want to give the defendant bail, if at all possible.

It is unwise to begin the application by mentioning factors which arouse sympathy for the defendant, such as the distress a remand in custody would give to her/his family. The magistrates are likely to feel: "That's all very well, but if we give this man bail, we'll never see him again."

It is generally better to deal first with the objections. The mere fact that the defence advocate treats them seriously and appears to have thought about how the objections may be overcome, carries weight. The court will then be more receptive to submissions on the rights and well-being of the defendant.

Unless the case is one in which you are fairly sure bail will be granted, do everything you can to make the application a duologue between the court and yourself. Lay magistrates tend to listen passively to advocates and then, after withdrawing for discussion, announce a decision. Before that announcement, the advocates have no indication as to which objection the bench is most concerned about. There are a number of techniques of making advocacy more a two-way process.

Example:
"I suspect, ma'am, that the court is more concerned about the possibility of absconding than about the possibility of further offending?"

This question has two advantages. If the answer is positive, you can confine your submissions to the absconding objections. Secondly, it forces the magistrates at this early stage to begin organising their thoughts about the application.

Example:
"Sir, I very much wish to avoid wasting court time. I wonder whether I can proceed on the basis that the court accepts that in principle Ms Jackson should have bail, subject to an acceptable address being found?"

This is not a suitable question to ask at the outset of an application; but after you have made submissions to the effect that in principle bail should be granted, it effectively asks whether the court accepts your argument so far. Even so, it is a quite bold question: you may well be told, No. But it is a very efficient question. If the answer is Yes, you have effectively got the court on your side—you need deal only with the ancillary problem of the address. If the answer is No, you could follow the question up with a second question to find out which objection the court is concerned about. You will be forcing the court into dialogue.

Example:
"Although I entirely accept it must be conditional, in my respectful submission, this is a case in which bail should be granted. I have endeavoured to address you, ma'am, on what I felt would be the court's principal concerns, but if the court has any lingering reservation about granting bail I shall be most happy to deal with it ..."

The most fundamental technique of advocacy is to make the tribunal feel uncomfortable in deciding against you.

If you state your case this strongly the court can either give your client bail, or indicate to you why it is unwilling to. It may be that the court's unwillingness is well-founded, and your client will not be bailed; but you will demonstrably have put her/his case as strongly as possible.

Before a stipendiary magistrate
Begin by stating what you are asking for.

Examples:
"Mr Perkins has been on unconditional police bail, sir, and I ask you to extend it to the next hearing."
"Ma'am, I ask you to give Mr Anifowoshe bail on three conditions: not to contact any prosecution witness directly or indirectly; not to go to the scene of the incident, The Red Lion pub, Hobson Street, Framley; and residence at his usual address, 16, Bede House, Eliot Street, Framley."

Almost certainly the stipendiary will either agree, or indicate her/his views.

Examples:
"Can he offer a surety?"
"This defendant has an extensive record of absconding. I don't think residence and reporting are a sufficient safeguard. I am minded to remand her in custody."

From the stipendiary's remarks you can infer what are her/his reservations in granting bail. If you think a condition suggested by the stipendiary would be acceptable to your client, or the stipendiary has raised an objection to bail which you think could be met by a condition acceptable to your client, ask the stipendiary for a brief moment to take instructions.

If you think your client will not be able to make a considered decision quickly, ask the stipendiary to put the case back in her/his list so you can take instructions in the cells. It should seldom happen that you need to take further instructions in a bail application. In preparation, you should consider all three objections, and take instructions on all possible conditions.

If your client is agreeable to the suggested condition(s) simply tell the magistrate that you ask her/him to grant bail on those terms. If the stipendiary proposes unacceptable conditions, or indicates an unwillingness to grant bail, proceed to address her/him on:

(a) the objection(s)
(b) the defendant's background as far as is relevant to that objection or condition
(c) possible bail conditions: either why the conditions s/he has suggested are unnecessary or impractical; or how the conditions you suggest will meet the bail objection.

In the unusual case where the stipendiary does not indicate her/his view at the outset, ask her/him whether s/he wishes you to address her/him on each of the objections raised by the prosecution, and proceed accordingly.

Taking a Surety

If your client's bail conditions include a surety, s/he will not be released until the surety has been taken either in court or at a police station.

If no-one is available at court, explain to your client that s/he should make arrangements for the prospective surety to attend any police station, taking with her/him proof of means.

If a proposed surety is present in court, call her/him to give evidence after the magistrates have granted bail.

Example:
"May the surety be taken now?"
"Certainly."
"I call Mr Patterson."
(Usher swears the surety)
"What is your full name? Address? What is your relationship to the defendant? Do you have [five hundred] pounds? Is it in a [building society] account? Is the account in your sole name? Do you realise that if the defendant fails to attend court punctually every time he is told to throughout the case you will almost certainly lose all of that money? How often do you see the defendant? Do you believe you have enough influence over him to make sure he attends court? Are you willing to stand surety for the defendant in the sum of [   ]

pounds? [To magistrate:] I don't know if the court has any questions for Mr Patterson?"

Practice varies in magistrates' courts. In some courts the clerk or a stipendiary magistrate will question the prospective surety; if the recognisance is small, the court may not require sight of the surety's passbook or statement of account.

ADJOURNMENT FOR PRE-SENTENCE REPORT

Before passing a community or custodial sentence, the court will normally adjourn for the preparation of a pre-sentence report. In the case of an adult, it may dispense with a report if the offence obviously calls for the type of sentence the court intends to pass; or if there is a recent report available to the court. In the case of a youth, the court may proceed without a new report only if a recent report is available.

Your client is likely to wish to be sentenced without adjournment for a report in the following situations:

(1) There is a recent, positive report so the obtaining of another report is unnecessary.

(2) You are able to persuade the court to deal with the defendant by way of a fine or conditional discharge.

(3) The court has indicated that it has in mind a short custodial sentence and is unwilling to grant the defendant bail while a report is prepared (a three-week remand in custody being equivalent to a six-week sentence).

(4) The defendant's wish to be sentenced by this particular bench (for example, because they have heard the evidence at trial) outweighs the possibility that a positive report may reduce the sentence.

In any other situation your client is likely to want a report to be prepared as its information about her/his circumstances and (following a Guilty plea only) the causes of her/his offending will provide the basis of the plea in mitigation.

MITIGATION OF SENTENCE

With a Pre-Sentence Report

First, establish the facts of the offence of which your client has been convicted. The more serious the offence, the more detail you require.

Form your own estimate of the likely sentence. Guidelines are given in Blackstone's, Archbold, and Anthony & Berryman. In beginning, you will probably be guided mainly by the pre-sentence report. Sentences are significantly higher in the Crown Court. The discount in sentence for a Guilty plea is less, the stronger the evidence against the defendant, with the least reduction for a defendant who was caught "red-handed".

The best mitigation is always previous good character.

Factors aggravating the offence:
Vulnerable victim
Having taken the lead
Victim a public servant *e.g.* bus driver, postman
Soiling, ransacking
Use of a weapon, especially one likely to cause serious injury
Professional hallmarks
Breach of trust
Premeditated offence
Property not recovered

Mitigating factors:
Being old
Being young
Receiving treatment (*e.g.* for substance dependence)
Having gained employment

Read the pre-sentence report, highlighting favourable passages, unfavourable passages and errors in three different colours. Consider the recommendation. Ask your client whether there are any inaccuracies in the report. Then advise her/him whether the recommendation is realistic and, if unrealistic, what is the likely sentence. Explain briefly what each sentence entails.

Types of Sentence

Probation order
The defendant will visit a Probation officer once per week for three months, then as often as directed. The Probation officer will discuss with the offender any specific problems (*e.g.* substance abuse; gambling; debts) and put the offender in touch with advisers on such problems, and discuss how the defendant can avoid future offending.

Community service
The defendant will work a specified number of hours without pay. S/he must turn up on time, every time, otherwise s/he will be brought back

to court for breach of the order and is likely to be sent to prison. Community service is an alternative to prison. If at any point in the order s/he is too ill to do the community service, s/he must phone the organiser, and obtain a doctor's certificate as soon as possible.

Combination order
This combines a probation order with a number of hours of community service.

Taking instructions
Ask your client what sentence s/he wants you to seek, and what would be second-best. If s/he has pleaded Guilty, obtain from her/him a detailed account of the offence; how s/he came to commit it; and how s/he feels about it now (*i.e.* whether s/he is sorry).

Then ask her/him a series of questions to elicit information about her/his background and circumstances. Explain that you will not mention any information against her/his wishes. Ask:

—at what age, and with what qualifications, s/he left school (only if s/he is under 30)
—whether s/he has any further education or vocational qualifications (again, only if under 30)
—about her/his recent employment history
—how s/he became unemployed, and what steps s/he has taken and is taking to obtain work
—when her/his present relationship began (or previous one ended)
—the ages of any children and whether any of them has special needs
—about hobbies/interests/social groups/church membership/ etc
—what s/he sees her/himself doing in five years' time (only under 30s)
—how s/he thinks s/he came to commit the offence (only if s/he pleaded Guilty)

Finally always obtain details of your client's means in case there is a fine, compensation or costs order. Ask her/his total weekly income; approximate figures for outgoings; how many people are dependent on that money; and what is left at the end of the week/fortnight. Convert all figures to weekly amounts to present to the court, but if the client is on benefit, ask that the fines, etc., can be paid fortnightly.

Pitching the mitigation
Sentencing is very inconsistent between different magistrates' courts (and not infrequently within a court), so it is inevitable that the best advocate will, from time to time, pitch the mitigation at a level different from that being considered by the magistrates.

Lay magistrates will generally be guided by the pre-sentence report.

Thus if you consider the PSR recommendation is unrealistically lenient, it is still worth asking the magistrates to implement it, although if they do, the actual sentence is likely to be heavy of its kind (*e.g.* a large fine, or a long community service order). You will have your work cut out in persuading the bench, and you will be well-advised to have an alternative proposal to suggest.

If you consider the PSR recommendation is too severe, have a word with the duty Probation officer in court. If s/he agrees with you, ask her/him whether another report could be prepared (the answer may well be No, but it is worth making sure). It may be that s/he will tell you that the offence in question is regarded very seriously in this court, and that sentences of the sort recommended are routinely passed.

If you are arguing for a more lenient sentence than that recommended in the PSR, do not directly challenge the appropriateness of the recommendation. Magistrates generally feel a sense of loyalty to the court's Probation officers and, secondly, it is always unattractive to sentencers to hear advocates appear to minimise the seriousness of the offence.

Two ways of dealing with an unfavourable PSR are, firstly, to mention factors (which may have been) unknown to the author of the report. For example, a recent offer of employment may make it far harder than the Probation officer would have envisaged to do community service (so a fine would be more appropriate). The unknown factors may be to do with the offence itself. There may be a number of mitigating factors arising from it which are not mentioned in the very general outline of the facts given in the report.

Another way is to endorse the findings of the Probation officer and use them as the basis for an argument for a different disposal. Whereas the Probation officer feels the seriousness of the offence necessitates a community sentence, despite personal mitigation, you might argue that the personal mitigation enables a financial penalty despite the seriousness of the offence. Never even imply that the Probation officer is wrong; simply argue positively for the sentence you want, making use of any helpful findings of the PSR.

Stipendiary magistrates (and Crown Court judges) may invariably refer to PSRs with respect, but they are much less guided by them. A stipendiary magistrate will usually tell you at the outset if s/he regards the report as unrealistic. In the (unlikely) event that s/he regards it as unrealistically severe, you may have little to do. However, you should be prepared to address the stipendiary on the basis that s/he considers the report unrealistically lenient.

If this should be the case, do not argue that the recommendation is realistic (the stipendiary has considered that argument and rejected it). Either draw to the stipendiary's attention matters that are not mentioned in the report and seek to persuade the stipendiary that in the light of all the information before her/him it is right to implement the recommendation. Alternatively, concede that the report's recommendation is unrealistic and argue for a different sentence.

It will nevertheless occasionally happen, generally with lay magistrates, that your mitigation is heard out in full, and then the magistrate tells you that you have misjudged the level of seriousness. If this should happen, ask the court for an indication of the sentence it has in mind, and ask for the case to be put back in the list for you to take further instructions.

If there is any intermediate ground between what you have asked for and what the magistrate has indicated (*e.g.* you sought a fine and the magistrate indicates custody) your client will almost certainly instruct you to aim for the middle option (*e.g.* a community sentence).

If there is no intermediate ground (*e.g.* you sought probation and the magistrate indicates custody) you will already have said everything there is to say in favour of the sentence you are contending for. Do not repeat it.

Make any points which you have not already made on the appropriate level of sentence. A good starting point is to begin by accepting that this sort of offence would normally attract custody (you should always begin every address to every tribunal at a point on which the tribunal and yourself are in agreement) but then give examples of "typical features" of such offences which are absent in this case, and refer to the fact that here there are a number of mitigating factors which you have already mentioned (do not repeat them).

Then tactfully argue, giving reasons, that the sentence proposed by the court will not meet its sentencing objectives.

Finally, submit that the sentence you are seeking would best achieve those objectives for the reasons you outlined earlier, and that if you can assist the court further you will be pleased to do so.

A Working Plan for a Speech in Mitigation

(1) *Establish that the magistrates have read the pre-sentence report*
If the magistrates indicate their agreement with the recommendation, do not address them further, except to inform them of your client's means, if relevant.

Example:
"I am most grateful. Unless I can assist the court further, there is nothing I wish to add."

(2) *Correct any inaccuracies in the report*

Example:
"There are two minor errors in the report. On page 2, the third

paragraph, beginning, 'When he was eight...', should read, 'two', not 'three' brothers.

"And on page 3, the fourth paragraph, beginning, 'After leaving school...', the eighth line, 'was not kept on at the end of his probationary period'; this was because, due to the recession, the firm was shedding staff; the defendant had successfully completed his probationary period."

(3) *Give details of the defendant's means*

Example:

"The defendant's average weekly earnings are £a; he receives £b in welfare benefits; a total weekly income of £c.

"He pays £d rent; weekly bills including food, come to £e.

"The defendant owes the gas company and catalogues £f, towards which he pays £g per week.

"At the end of the week, therefore, he is left with [£c—(£d + £e + £g) =] £h for himself, his girlfriend and their two children."

(4) *Indicate the sentence you are asking the court to pass*

(5) *Address the court on the facts of the offence, dealing with any aggravating features, and drawing out mitigating ones*
You must not address the court on a basis inconsistent with the defendant's plea; nor must you cast doubt on facts which have been found proved.

(6) *Submit either (a) that the seriousness of the offence is commensurate with the sentence you are advocating; or (b) that although the offence itself would merit a heavier sentence, mitigation personal to the defendant enables the court to pass the sentence you are advocating*

(7) *Address the court on the defendant's circumstances*
Work to the pattern:

Problem
Offence
Sentence
Happy ending

(8) *"For these reasons, I ask the court to.... unless I can assist the court further, those are my submissions."*

Pleading in Mitigation

An advocate who addresses a court in mitigation of sentence has the opportunity to prepare her/his submissions in advance, and is usually heard out in silence by a court genuinely seeking assistance as to the fairest sentence to pass.

Despite these advantages, it is unusual to hear a good speech in mitigation in the magistrates' court. Many speeches are as much in aggravation as mitigation and often give the impression of having been made many times before by advocates who cannot be bothered to make them yet again.

This is partly the fault of magistrates who listen passively to whatever is said rather than giving the advocate any indication of what it would assist them to be addressed on. But the principal problem is the lack of structure in the speeches.

Always begin by indicating the sentence you are asking the court to pass. This most basic rule is routinely broken by advocates who launch directly into a narrative of the background and personal problems of their client, prompting the listener at one moment to think the advocate must be recommending a probation order for a defendant with so many problems, then to think the advocate is seeking to avoid a fine, because of the defendant's poverty, finally to discover that the advocate is seeking a conditional discharge and compensation order. State your object at the outset, and the magistrates will then be primed to pick up points in favour of that disposal.

The following are stock beginnings:

Examples:

"May it please you, ma'am; I ask you to implement the recommendation of the pre-sentence report for these reasons..."

"May it please you, sir; I shall seek to persuade the court that the right disposal of this case is a community service order..."

"May it please you, ma'am; although I of course accept that this offence is, as the pre-sentence report says, one serious enough to merit a community sentence, I shall seek to persuade you that the particular circumstances of the defendant are such as to enable you to deal with this case by way of a fine."

Address the court on the assumption that it is trying to inflict the least punishment on the defendant consistent with its duty to vindicate the law.

Always address the court argumentatively: give reasons why the aggravating features of the offence do not necessitate a heavy sentence, and demonstrate how all the circumstances logically propel one in the direction of the sentence you are arguing for.

The underlying technique is to make the court feel uncomfortable in passing a sentence heavier than the one you are contending for. It follows from this that you must be proposing a realistic sentence.

Another aspect of the technique is that you should imply: "Everyone else thinks as I do". One way of doing this is to quote sentencing guidelines or decided cases (the implication being: the Court of Appeal says a community sentence is appropriate in this sort of case). Another way is to emphasize the thought the Probation officer has put into her/his report ("You may think this is a thorough and considered report").

Pointing out the presence of relatives in court has the same effect. If everyone present in court is, seemingly, awaiting a merciful *but wise* sentence, it is difficult for the magistrates to disappoint this expectation.

One straight-forward and adaptable structure for your speech is to deal first with the facts of the offence, then the circumstances of the defendant (this order is generally followed in pre-sentence reports).

If the defendant had pleaded Not Guilty, you are restricted in what you can say about the facts of the case to what has been proved. You may, for example, say, "All the goods were recovered" or "In opening the case the learned prosecutor said, 'Bloggins played a minor role'". The rule is that you cannot put forward in mitigation anything inconsistent with the plea of Not Guilty.

Examples:
In an identification case you can say virtually nothing beyond the facts proved, because it was the defendant's case that s/he was not there at all. S/he cannot, therefore (through you) now say, for example, "The victim had been very verbally offensive and insulting which made the defendant lose her temper."

In a defence of self-defence case you cannot say, "The defendant for a moment lost his temper and lashed out at the Victim which he now regrets" (but you are entitled to say: "The defendant very much regrets that he did not leave the Victim's shop as soon as the argument started" as this is not inconsistent with the defendant's account that he believed the Victim was about to attack him [or had attacked him]).

In a shop lifting case you cannot say "It was a momentary impulse". In a case of driving without due care it is inappropriate to apologise for bad driving.

Secondly, you must not cast doubt upon facts which have been found proved.

Examples:
"...the Victim has exaggerated the number of blows ..."
"...speed not so high as the police officers said ..."

Where your client has been convicted upon evidence called, only make points on the facts which are clearly based upon the prosecution case and are significant for sentencing purposes.

It will generally be useful to make a realistic comment as to the level of seriousness of the offence.

Examples:
"In my submission this case is towards the less serious end of the range of 'without due care'."
"I am very mindful of the fact that this was an attack on a bus driver at a time of late evening when few people were around ..."

The purpose of mentioning that the case you are mitigating is a bad case of its kind, is to imbue your address to the court with an air of realism. If you make no mention of the seriousness of the offence, it will be easier for the magistrates to write off what you say; whereas the approach "This is a bad case... nevertheless... taking everything into account I submit the correct disposal is... ", carries weight.

But do take great care not to say anything which will make the offence seem worse than the prosecution indicated it was. You will quite often hear advocates do this.

An advantage to the defendant of pleading Guilty is that in mitigation you can give her/his account both of how s/he came to commit the offence and of what happened. In giving that account, do not state a version of events which is crudely favourable to the defendant; give a neutral account, but pick your words with great care to convey the impression you want.

Example:
'The Victim and the defendant had exchanged verbal insults, then the defendant punched the Victim in the face.

Do not say:

"The Victim made a number of offensive and insulting remarks to the defendant who, goaded beyond endurance, stuck him in the face."

But:

"After a brief exchange of verbal insults it was the defendant who struck the Victim."

It is implied, rather than stated, that it could just as easily have been the other way around. Wherever possible, provide the material facts which make a favourable inference starkly obvious—but do not draw the inference yourself. A conclusion will carry more weight with the magistrates if arrived at by themselves, than if suggested by you.

Always make it clear to the court that the defendant is sorry for the offence (if you are so instructed).

In dealing with the facts of the offence you should always have an unstated "explanatory label" in mind.

Examples:
"six of one, half a dozen of the other"
"boyish mischief"
"easily led"
Road traffic: "act of momentary inattention"

Similarly, in dealing with the defendant's circumstances the pattern "Problem, Offence, Sentence, Happy ending" should not be explicit.

Examples:
The defendant's drink problem led him to steal. A probation order will stop him drinking and offending.
The rather immature young defendant has not had a job since he left school a year ago. He has become bored, and has no money to pursue any interests, and has drifted into a number of offences, including the present quite minor matter of criminal damage. He has now gained employment, so a conditional discharge will serve as a "sword of Damocles" to keep him out of trouble while he finds his feet in the adult world.

In dealing with the defendant's circumstances you are simultaneously attempting two objects: gaining the sympathy of the magistrates for your client so they will want to inflict upon her/him as little punishment as possible. This operates at an emotional level.

Secondly, convincing the magistrates that your client will respond positively to the least restrictive sentence, so that they can justify to themselves imposing the minimal punishment. This operates at a rational level. In attempting this combined task your stock-in-trade is a collection of stereotypical characters and stories.

Examples:
"the respectable person who has made one lapse" (no previous record and has offended only because of exceptional circumstances)
"the addict" (would not offend except for her/his addiction)
"the easily led" (offends only because of the influence of others)
"the desperate for work" (would not offend if only s/he had a job)

You should attempt always to attribute offending behaviour to circumstances, because attribution to the defendant's character reduces the magistrates' sympathy for her/him, and makes them less hopeful of her/his positive response.

You should always stress the defendant's social respectability.

Examples:
Employment; educational achievement or endeavour or aspiration; marriage; parenthood; religious observation; home ownership

The more the magistrates feel the defendant is basically like themselves (or their children) the more sympathetic they will be towards her/him and hopeful of her/his positive response.

It is customary for the magistrates to read the pre-sentence report before being addressed in mitigation. Always address them on the assumption that they have read every word. Never state a fact which is stated in the report unless you have very good reason to, and then always acknowledge the repetition (*e.g.* "as you have read").

Finally, there are a number of stock mitigating factors: previous good character; plea of guilty at the first opportunity; all goods recovered; full admissions; and, co-operative with the police.

It will usually be unnecessary to mention any of them because they are mentioned or are implicit in the facts opened by the prosecutor. If it is desirable to deal with any of them do so in as few words as possible. The magistrates are extremely familiar with all of these factors, and used to giving appropriate credit for them.

Two Variations:

(i) No pre-sentence report
If a pre-sentence report is not available, having been ordered, the court will adjourn the case for a report to be prepared, unless there is no report because the defendant failed to attend for interview. If that is the reason, explain to the court why s/he did not attend, and ask for the case to be adjourned to give her/him another opportunity to be interviewed.

If there is no PSR because the defendant has just been convicted or pleaded Guilty, the court must decide whether it needs a report before passing sentence. The circumstances in which you would seek to persuade the court to sentence without a report are outlined at page 144. If the magistrates indicate they require a report, your mitigation can begin in these terms:

Example I:
"Sir; I seek to persuade you to deal with this offence this afternoon by way of a fine.
"I of course accept that this is an offence for which the court would first consider a community sentence.

"I seek to persuade the court that factors personal to the defendant—
and I have full instructions as to her personal circumstances—justify
the court in dealing with the offence by way of a fine. If I fail to
persuade the court of that, then, of course, I accept the case will have
to go over for a report ..."

Example II:
"Ma'am; I seek to persuade the court that this particular offence falls
short, perhaps only just short, of meriting a community sentence. If I
fail, then of course I accept the case will have to be adjourned for a
pre-sentence report ..."

Modify the working plan for a speech in mitigation (see page 148) in
this way:

A Working Plan for Mitigation without a Report

(3) *Give details of the defendant's means*
These will invariably be relevant.

(4) *Indicate the sentence you are asking the court to pass*

(5a) *(If the court has heard evidence:) Refer only very briefly to any
mitigating factors in the evidence the court has just heard*
or

(5b) *(If the defendant has pleaded Guilty:) Address the court on the
facts of the offence, dealing with any aggravating features, and
drawing out mitigating ones*

(6) *Submit either (a) that the offence is not serious enough to justify
a community sentence, but can be dealt with by a conditional
discharge or fine; or (b) that although the offence itself would
merit a community sentence, mitigation personal to the defendant
enables the court to deal with it by way of a conditional discharge
or fine*

(7) *Address the court on the circumstances of the defendant*
Work to the pattern:

Problem
Offence
Sentence
Happy ending

(8) *"For these reasons, I ask the court to....unless I can assist the
court further, those are my submissions."*

(ii) Preparation in advance

When a case you are dealing with is adjourned for a pre-sentence
report (see page 144), consider the following matters:

Character witnesses

The Rumpolean dictum that calling the curate to testify to the better side of the defendant's character can be relied on to add six months to the sentence may be true at the Old Bailey: magistrates' courts have more respect for the cloth, and for persons of social position generally.

Character witnesses are very seldom called, but there are very few cases in which a well-chosen character witness from whom a statement has been carefully taken would not assist both the court and the defendant.

The witness should be someone who has known the defendant either for a long time, or very well, or in some specialist capacity. An employer will generally be an effective character witness because s/he has daily contact with the defendant, yet is not a relative or friend and demonstrates her/his confidence in the defendant by continuing to employ her/him. The fact that s/he has given up the time to come to court speaks for itself.

The witness's evidence should not be a catalogue of the defendant's good points: it should be closely tied in with your argument in mitigation.

Example I:

Argument: the defendant had unacknowledged alcohol dependency. The offence was committed in drink. The defendant is now full of remorse and is currently not drinking. A probation order would help him fully acknowledge his problem and deal with the reasons for it, reinforced by the knowledge that any further offending during the period of the order will not be viewed leniently.

Character evidence: the witness works in a voluntary alcohol abuse project from whom the defendant sought help soon after the offence; he has received regular counselling, and has a plan for sensible drinking.

Example II:

Argument: the defendant has been under a great deal of pressure because of difficulty in caring for a handicapped child. The offence was totally out of character. Prison would cause great pressure on the defendant's spouse, and distress to the whole family.

Character evidence: the witness has known the defendant for many years, remembers what fun she used to be, the voluntary work she did, etc, the great distress over the child's handicap, the feelings of guilt and the fact the defendant was torn between feeling she should work long hours to earn money for the family and feeling she should spend more time with the children.

References and written job offers

Many applicants for bail, even those who have been unemployed for years, give instructions that they are just about to start a new job which a remand in custody would prevent. The same is true of those about to be sentenced.

The reality of such a job is greatly enhanced by the production of a written offer. Always advise a client to bring such a letter with her/him to court or, ideally, to take it to her/his solicitor to have photocopies made.

If a defendant is in employment, a written reference from her/his employer will carry weight with the court.

The pre-sentence report

Advise your client what sentences are realistic. Discuss her/his circumstances with her/him and point out any mitigating factors. Tell her/him it is up to her/him to mention them to the Probation officer. S/he should ask the Probation officer what the report's recommendation will be and, if it is a sentence s/he does not want, should try to persuade the Probation officer to change it.

Explain to her/him that the pre-sentence report carries much weight in the magistrates' court.

Time

Explain to your client that on the next court date her/his case may be the first one to be called on, and so to prepare adequately you will arrive at court one hour before the court sits, and so should s/he.

PROSECUTING A REMAND LIST

Preparation

With each file, first establish the stage the case has reached by reference to the flow-diagram on page 158.

On your copy of the court list, against the name of each case, put one of the following codes:

SEN	Case is for sentence
PLEA	All charges are summary, prosecution are ready for plea to be entered
SERVE AI	Advance information is on file
MoT	Advance information has been served, prosecution are ready for Mode of Trial
ADJ	Prosecution seek adjournment

Check the file contains the following:

Antecedents (Previous convictions, "form MG16")
Brief facts (Summary of evidence)
Compensation claim form (if relevant)
Dates to avoid for all prosecution witnesses

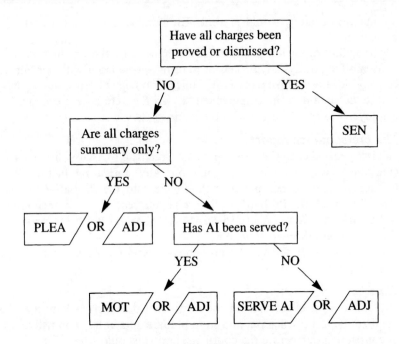

All of these are needed for every case, except that Dates to Avoid are not needed if (i) the case has already been proved or (ii) the charges are indictable only. If anything is missing, note it on a memo sticker on the front of the file and in a memo to the reviewing lawyer.

If the case is ready for Mode of Trial, the prosecution view on the appropriate court will be marked on the front of the file at the top right: either "SST" (suitable for summary trial) or "NSST" (not suitable) will have been circled.

In the rare case where the prosecution view is not marked, check the inside back cover ("page 3") of the file. If there is no indication, consider the facts of the case in the light of the Mode of Trial Guidelines (in Stone's and Blackstone's) and form your own view. Make a note on a "Problems" sheet that you need instructions.

Read the most recent letter from defence solicitors, and check that any points it raises have been dealt with (for example, if the letter indicates the defendant will plead Guilty to two of three charges, is there an endorsement to indicate whether this is acceptable?; if there is a request for copies of witness statements in a summary case, is there an endorsement to indicate whether these are to be provided?). If there are any points which have not been dealt with, note them on your "Problems" sheet.

When you have prepared all the files, check your court list to ensure there is an endorsement against each name. Note any missing file on your "Problems" sheet.

Before Court

Deal first with any missing files, and take instructions on any problems (acceptability of pleas, views on Mode of Trial, etc.). Then prepare any overnights. Check that each has a Form MG7; if it is missing, consider why the police have refused to release the defendant on bail. It will usually be because of the seriousness of the offence; the lack of a fixed home; or a record of previous failures to surrender.

When defence advocates arrive, deal with the following matters:

SEN   If you anticipate there may be a dispute on the facts, indicate the prosecution version. Show the advocate any compensation claim form

PLEA   Show the defence the "brief facts" (summary of evidence) or the witness statements. If the intention is to plead Not Guilty see if you can get agreement that part of the evidence (*e.g.* a loser's statement) can be read section 9

SERVE AI   Give the defence the AI

MoT   Inform the defence of the prosecution's view on the appropriate court

ADJ   Explain why the prosecution are seeking an adjournment

In Court

First appearance: summary only
Indicate you are ready for the charge to be put.

If the plea is Guilty, proceed to sentence, as below.

If it is Not Guilty, state the number of prosecution witnesses and indicate dates to avoid in the month the court can offer trial.

If the defendant has been on bail, state that there is no objection to unconditional bail or bail on the same terms, as appropriate.

If the defendant appears in custody, pass a copy of her/his previous convictions to the defence advocate, ask if it is agreed, and hand it up to the bench. If the convictions are not agreed, indicate that to the court and endorse the file for them to be verified before the next hearing. State which of the four objections to bail (failure to surrender; likelihood of committing further offences; interference with witnesses; for her/his own protection) apply; and support those objections with information from the form MG7.

First appearance: either-way offence

If the defence request Advance Information, seek a two-week adjournment for it to be prepared. Deal with bail, as above.

If the defence do not seek AI, proceed to Mode of Trial, as below.

Mode of Trial

Indicate whether the prosecution say the case is suitable or unsuitable for summary trial, and support that representation either by indicating the relevant aggravating features or their absence.

If jurisdiction is declined, proceed to deal with bail, as above.

If jurisdiction is retained and the defendant pleads Guilty, proceed to sentence, as below.

If the defendant pleads Not Guilty, proceed to set a trial date and deal with bail, as above.

Sentence

Outline the brief facts. Deal with the four C's. Pass a copy of the defendant's previous Convictions to the defence advocate, ask if it is agreed, and hand it up to the bench. Apply, if appropriate, for Compensation, and Confiscation (forfeiture or destruction orders for weapons and drugs); and seek a contribution to prosecution Costs.

All hearings

Finally, and most importantly, make sure you have fully and legibly endorsed the file so that everyone who deals with it subsequently can see easily what happened at the hearing. In particular, make sure that it is clear:

—whether the defendant attended

—whether s/he was represented

—on what terms bail was granted

—whether the defendant met those terms (*e.g.* provided any surety specified)

—why the case was adjourned, (*e.g.* for sentence; to prepare AI; for trial; etc).

If there is more than one defendant, it is important to make it clear in respect of each:

(i) the date of the next hearing, and

(ii) why the case has been adjourned

or:

how the case against that defendant has been disposed of, (*e.g.* NEO [no evidence offered]; withdrawn; sentenced; etc).

CHAPTER 5

CIVIL HEARINGS

CIVIL TRIAL

Begin by reading the Particulars/Statement of Claim. Note (a) the plaintiff's cause of action, (b) what s/he must prove and (c) what remedies s/he seeks.

Example I:
Negligence—driving
Pl: that the accident was caused by Def.'s negligent driving
Remedy: damages

Example II:
Contract—debt
Pl: that Def. ordered equipment; Pl delivered equipment; Pl billed Def.; Def. has not paid
Remedy: damages

Briefly consider the law, and the Particulars of Claim. With this cause of action is the plaintiff entitled to the remedy s/he seeks? Is anything missing from the Particulars of Claim (example: in a nuisance case, does the plaintiff state what is her/his interest in the land?) Has interest been claimed? Read the defence (and any counterclaim), and incorporate it in your notes.

Example I:

Negligence—driving Pl: accident was caused by Def.'s negligent driving	Def.: accident caused by Pl's negligent driving
Remedy: damages	Remedy: no counterclaim [note: Def. may seek to amend]

Example II:

Contract—debt Pl: Def ordered equipment Pl: delivered equipment	Def.: agreed Pl: delivered wrong equipment incompatible with Def.'s system

Pl billed Def	agreed
Put to proof	Def. lost 7 days' production, worth £x
Remedy: damages (£y claimed)	Remedy: damages (£x claimed)

Note the areas of dispute between the parties, and then "brainstorm" the evidence you would ideally like on both sides.

Example I:

Negligence—driving
Both parties:
independent witnesses—partisan witnesses—forensic evidence, *e.g.* skidmarks, glass on road—police accident report— report of damage to vehicles—photographs of road—sketchplan

Example II:

Contract—debt
order note—note of conversation—information as to when Def notified Pl that equipment was wrong—information as to whether (and when and where from) Def obtained correct equipment—price paid for it— why Def could not have obtained it within the 7 days—information as to why execution of the order could not have been delayed

Read the plaintiff's evidence very carefully, listing:

   (i) any of your questions which are not answered in the plaintiff's evidence
  (ii) any further questions which her/his evidence suggests
 (iii) any gaps in the plaintiff's evidence

Then note down the points for and against the plaintiff. Read the defendant's evidence, noting the same questions and points. Re-read the pleadings to ensure your case is correctly pleaded, and to note whether the other side's case requires amendment.

Up to this point your preparation should have been non-partisan, considering the plaintiff's and defendant's cases impartially.

Now that you are clear what the issues are, make sure that you understand thoroughly the applicable law. If there are any cases to which you may wish to refer the judge, make three copies of each. Now consider your case.

The Claimant's Case

(The plaintiff or counterclaiming defendant's case)

All advocacy works, to some extent, on two levels. They may be labelled in various ways (intellectual/gut; evidential/empathetic; head/heart) and are referred to here as the "legal case" and the "moral case".

The legal case is primary. It consists of the cause of action/defence; the factual points the party must prove to make out her/his case/defence; and the evidence on those points. The case is opened in terms of the legal case, and the closing speech argues that the party's legal case has been made out.

Example I:
Ancillary relief
Dispute: level of settlement

Petitioner's legal case: she has two young children to care for; cannot work full-time; her earning capacity has been curtailed by childcare responsibilities; the respondent has good earning capacity
Respondent's legal case: he has to rehouse himself; his earnings are unlikely to increase; the petitioner's needs are lessened in that she can share domestic expenses with her co-habitee

Example II:
Personal injury
Dispute: liability and quantum

Plaintiff's legal case: slipped on greasy floor; injury to knee, initially acutely painful; eight weeks off work; unable to play football and some difficulty in lifting and carrying
Respondent's legal case: some degree of contributory negligence; could have returned to work sooner; present degree of incapacity exaggerated

Example III:
Landlord and tenant
Dispute: lease or licence?

Landlord's legal case: this was a temporary arrangement; the written agreement shows it is a licence; it was freely signed by the tenant
Tenant's legal case: there was no time limit on her occupancy of the accommodation; the landlord told her it was necessary for the written agreement to state "licence" because of his legal position, but she was welcome to stay as long as she liked

In all trials where facts as well as law are in dispute, each party's legal case is underpinned by a moral one. The moral case comprises those social stereotypes and stock explanations of behaviour which make the legal case intelligible.

Example I:
Ancillary relief

Petitioner's moral case: she is only trying to do her best for their children; the respondent wants to run away from his responsibilities
Respondent's moral case: his earnings since the elder child's birth have largely been spent on the family; the petitioner has now moved another man into the family home; if the settlement is too much the respondent will be left without home as well as without family

Example II:
Personal injury

Plaintiff's moral case: the plaintiff is an ordinary man in the street who has had an accident and the faceless insurance company is trying to welch on its responsibilities
Defendant's moral case: it has always accepted the plaintiff is entitled to compensation, but he is milking a comparatively minor accident for all it is worth

Example III:
Landlord and tenant

Landlord's moral case: he tried to help someone and has been as above-board as possible, and she is trying to exploit the situation
Tenant's moral case: she had no choice but to sign the sham licence agreement, but the landlord is going back on the real agreement

The trial is, on one level, a number of disputes about specific parts of the evidence; at another level it is a contest between opposing moral cases.

·Alternatively, the "moral case" can be seen as meaning nothing more than "credibility", the basis upon which the judge decides which evidence s/he accepts and rejects, and so decides the legal case. It is, anyway, necessary to pay attention to both aspects. List the points of the legal case which you need to prove, and the evidence on each point. Note down the moral case and list the evidence for it.

Example I:
Ancillary relief

Petitioner's moral case
Evidence: her spending on the children, lack of spending on herself; the respondent's lack of contact with his children since the separation

Respondent's moral case
Evidence: his past spending on the family; lack of spending on himself; the speed with which the co-habitee moved into the matrimonial home; his present lack of means

Example II:
Personal injury

Plaintiff's moral case
Evidence: his ordinariness, married with children, enjoyment of family life, football with children, shopping trips

Respondent's moral case
Evidence: shortly after accident, plaintiff said it hurt "only for a moment"; his accounts of how much football he played prior to the accident are unconvincing

Example III:
Landlord and tenant

Landlord's moral case
Evidence: family connection with the tenant, urgency of tenant's need for housing

Tenant's moral case
Evidence: there was no mention of the licence between her moving in and her asking for repairs to be done

Example IV:
Negligence—driving

Plaintiff's legal case: the defendant's car emerged from a junction into her path causing a collision
Plaintiff's moral case: she is a careful, experienced driver, and the defendant an impatient, inexperienced young man
Evidence: the plaintiff's age; the fact she has been a driver over forty years; she has never had points on her licence; no insurance claims; the youth of the defendant

Example V:
Contract—debt

Plaintiff's legal case: the equipment was supplied to the defendant who has refused to pay
Plaintiff's moral case: it is an efficient company which has supplied equipment to the defendant on many previous occasions, and it fulfilled this order promptly. The defendant is a disorganised company which over-optimistically ordered equipment it could not afford and now cannot pay for. Despite alleging that the plaintiff supplied the wrong equipment, the defendant has not ordered different equipment from the plaintiff or anyone else
Evidence: the documentation of the large number of the defendant's

orders which the plaintiff has fulfilled; the conversancy of the plaintiff's orders manager with the defendant's business, its equipment and needs; the fact that in the defendant's original defence the "correct" equipment allegedly needed was wrongly identified; the absence of any purchase by the defendant of the "correct" equipment

Plan your speech. Your argument is that the evidence as a whole makes your client's version of events more credible than the defendant's. Consider how you will deal with those parts of the evidence which are adverse.

The Defendant's Case
(The defendant's or counterclaimed-against plaintiff's case)

List the points the claimant needs to prove to win her/his case. Has s/he got evidence on each of the points? How much of the claimant's case do you want to dispute? If you accept the claimant's case on all but one point, that point may appear to the judge more genuinely challenged than if you put the claimant to proof on everything. By making admissions as to some parts of the claimant's case, you may preclude evidence which, if given, would be very damaging to your case.

Conversely, it may be as well to put the claimant to proof on a disputed point on which you anticipate losing, because although the claimant's evidence will assist her/his legal case, it will do greater damage to her/his moral case.

Plan your speech. Your argument is likely to be either (i) that the evidence as a whole makes your client's version of events more credible than the claimant's, or (ii) that on one crucial point your client's evidence is to be preferred.

If the case is such that one party will win outright, calculate any interest which will be claimed.

The Bundle

Unless you have been provided with one, make a bundle of documents if you have time. It is at this stage too late to agree a bundle, so if you are representing the defendant it is better to take your own, than have none.

Arrange each document which you want the judge to see in chronological order. When you are certain you have included everything you need in the right order, prominently number each page (not each document) and write out an index, which goes at the front.

Example:

pp 1–3		Particulars of Claim
4–5		Defence
6	17/5/95	Letter Def > Pl
7	22/5/95	Reply Pl > Def
8	25/5/95	Pl's telephone memo
9	26/5/95	Def's order
10	28/5/95	Pl's acknowledgment

Then put the pile of documents through the photocopier, making three identical copies (for your opponent, the witness, and yourself; the judge has the original).

Consider a Settlement

If there is no case in law
In considering the pleadings (see pages 161 to 162), you will have checked that there is in law both a valid claim and a valid defence. If you represent a claimant with no valid claim in law (or a defendant with no valid defence) you need to either amend or settle. It may therefore be well worth considering on what terms it would be advantageous to settle, rather than possibly incur costs in amending, obtaining further evidence, and so on.

If you represent the defendant/claimant to an invalid claim/defence, do not begin negotiations to settle. If your opponent attempts to negotiate, do not settle (you are bound to win).

If your opponent indicates the invalidity of her/his claim/defence and says s/he is seeking an amendment, it may be advantageous to your client to settle.

If the amendment would genuinely cause difficulty to your client (for example, it would make desirable the obtaining of further evidence) the judge is likely to adjourn the case and order the other side to pay the costs thrown away. The other side, therefore, has a strong incentive to settle. It is therefore worthwhile considering on what terms it may be advantageous to both parties to settle rather than come back another day.

If the amendment will not cause difficulties to the other side (in a relatively simple case it is unlikely to) the judge will almost certainly give leave to amend without an adjournment.

If the evidence is very weak
If the other side's evidence is very weak, it is very likely that your opponent will attempt to negotiate a settlement. Be prepared. If you

have thoroughly and dispassionately considered both sides' evidence, you will not be tempted to feel there may be advantages in the certainty of a settlement.

If it is your evidence which is weak, consider possible terms for settlement.

Before the hearing

No matter how short of time you are, always spend a few minutes reassuring your client and her/his witnesses and explaining the court procedure to them (see page 25).

Take a proof of evidence from each witness separately (see pages 23 to 25). If witness statements have previously been taken (and exchanged with the other side), take a supplementary statement dealing only with those questions which occurred to you after you read the main statements. In taking the supplementary statements you should form a view as to whether each witness's evidence will come over better from the witness box or on paper.

Discuss the conduct of the case with your lay client. In a relatively simple case (*e.g.* a road traffic accident) this will not be necessary. In a more complex case, there may be tactical decisions to take about how the case is put.

Negotiation and settlement

The reason why it is nearly always better to settle any civil case if you possibly can, is the saving in costs.

In a relatively simple case there is no overall costs saving in settling at the door of the court. Generally, therefore, it is not a good idea to suggest to your client that s/he instruct you to negotiate with the other side. Inevitably it conveys the impression you feel s/he has a weak case, which in turn may lead her/him to consider settling at a level s/he would not have otherwise thought of.

If your client asks whether you think you should try to negotiate a settlement, ask her/him one or two questions to understand fully her/his position, and then advise her/him as fully as you can.

If your opponent approaches you to negotiate, tell her/him you have no instructions to do so; listen to any proposals s/he makes and then take instructions from your client.

If you had formed the impression that your client's case was evidentially weak, obviously you will advise that the opportunity to negotiate is to be taken seriously. Otherwise, it is largely a question of whether your client prefers the certainty of settlement to the risk of trial.

Opening the Plaintiff's Case

A cardinal rule in advocacy is "Never say what your client wants you to say; always what your tribunal wants to hear".

In preparing an address to any court, especially an opening, always consider what you will say from the point of view of the tribunal. If the judge has read the pleadings, do not repeat their contents to her/him. Correspondingly, if s/he has read none of the documents, do not assume any knowledge of the case. If you do not know whether s/he has read a document, ask.

Aim to open the case by giving the judge every piece of information s/he needs (and not a single piece s/he does not need) in exactly the most convenient order.

Take care with your opening, and the rest of the case will take care of itself.

Working Plan of Opening of Plaintiff's Case
(1) *Introduction*
     Introduce the parties and outline the issue(s) in one sentence.

Example:
"May it please your Honour; I appear for the plaintiff, my friend Ms Crabcheese appears for the first defendant, and my friend Mr Kumar appears for the second defendant.
"The plaintiff's claim is for damages arising out of a road traffic accident caused by the negligence of either or both defendants."

(2) *Offer to read the pleadings*
     Judges virtually always prefer to read the pleadings themselves, but it is polite to offer to read them.

Example:
"The Particulars of Claim were filed on the 3rd February; the Defence of the second defendant on the 2nd March; and the Defence of the first defendant on the 26th April. Might I assist your Honour by reading the pleadings?"

(3) *Deal with any proposed amendments*

Example:
"Your Honour will have noticed the Particulars of Claim are deficient in that no interest in the land is pleaded. With your Honour's leave I will amend the Particulars, and my friend kindly tells me he has no objection. The amendment I seek is the addition of a new sentence at the end of paragraph 2: "The plaintiff was at all material times..."

Example II:
"My friend Ms Cartwright wishes to amend the first defendant's defence to include a counterclaim, and neither Mr Snodgrass nor I have any objection." [Sits]

(4) *Indicate what is in issue*

Example I:
"The issue, of course, is whose negligence caused this accident."

Example II:
"There is no dispute that the defendant's survey was negligent; the only issue is whether that admitted negligence caused loss to the plaintiff."

Example III:
"The issue is whether this contract is on the plaintiff's or the defendant's standard terms."

(5) *Outline the plaintiff's version of the facts*
See the discussion on page 73 of the advantages of opening "high" or "low".

(6) *Outline your contention on any disputed point of law*
At this stage do not argue for your point of view or cite authority, simply state what you say are the legal consequences of your client's version of the facts.

(7) *Outline the remedy the plaintiff is seeking*
Indicate to the judge whether or not there is a dispute as to quantum.

Example I:
"The quantum of damages on both sides is agreed as pleaded, subject to liability."

Example II:
"The quantum of damages is not agreed. The plaintiff's car was repaired by Rippoff Mechanics, and the plaintiff will produce their receipted invoice in the sum of £x."

(8) *Outline the plaintiff's evidence*
Indicate who will be called and what documents will be put in evidence.

(9) *"With your Honour's leave, I will call the evidence. I call Mr Wong ..."*

Opening the Defendant's Case

The general rule is not to open unless there is a specific reason to. In a relatively simple case the judge will have gathered the defendant's case from the Defence and the cross-examination of the plaintiff's witnesses. Only if you feel the judge may not be fully aware of what the case is, or you feel a defence witness may be unclear in her/his evidence, should you open, and then do so very briefly.

Evidence-in-Chief (of either party)

You may call your evidence in whatever seems the most convenient order (there is no rule that your client must testify first).

The judge may decide to read the witness statements in place of examination-in-chief. If so, the witness should take the oath; you should then ask her/his name and address and (if relevant to her/his evidence) occupation; then pass her/him the signed original statement plus a copy and ask her/him whether that is her/his original statement; and true to the best of her/his knowledge and belief. Then ask for it to be handed up to the judge.

When the judge has read the statement, ask the witness any supplementary questions you have (see page 168).

If the parties have exchanged witness statements and you feel your case comes over better on paper (see page 168), you might suggest to the judge that s/he may prefer to read the statements in place of examination-in-chief.

Questioning

The judge will not take kindly to a refusal to allow leading questions on non-contentious matters. In the absence of a specific reason, do not refuse to allow your opponent to lead. There should not, therefore, be any difficulty in getting started. If there is, use the techniques outlined on pages 77–80.

If her/his evidence is relatively brief, allow the witness to tell her/his own story. If it is more complex, use a series of prompts, see pages 81 to 86.

You should aim to lead on everything that is not in dispute, and the trial will proceed more smoothly if you have previously shown your opponent a copy of the witness statement with the passages on which you intend to lead bracketed.

Cross-Examination

A broad generalisation is that a defence advocate alleges prosecution witnesses are mistaken; a prosecutor accuses defendants and their witnesses of lying.

The stance of a civil advocate may be at any point on that continuum, from a road traffic accident case where one alleges that the other driver has got the facts quite simply wrong, to a contract case where one accuses the other party of lying to evade liability.

Cross-examination in a civil case is more akin to prosecution cross-examination than defence because in both prosecution and civil cases one is putting to opposing witnesses a case one is trying to prove (in a civil trial, challenging the other party's case and putting one's own case generally come to the same thing). By contrast, in criminal defence, cross-examination is often limited to casting doubt on the prosecution case, without asserting very much as an alternative.

The general approach is that used in prosecution cross-examination. The judge will hear (or read) two conflicting accounts of what happened. What are the reasons for preferring your client's version?

Example I:
Negligence—driving

The defendant's case is that he was stationary at a junction waiting to emerge, when the plaintiff's car crossed the stop-line and hit his car.
Argument: Point 1: the junction is on a sudden, sharp, partially-concealed bend in the road; Point 2: the plaintiff is unfamiliar with the road; Point 3: the defendant's car was behind the stop-line when the police attended the accident.

Example II:
Contract—debt

The defendant's case is that the plaintiff supplied the wrong equipment; the defendant notified the plaintiff as soon as possible; the defendant has lost not only an order but, effectively, a client because of not having the equipment.
Argument: Point 1: the defendant had received a tentative order from a third party; Point 2: to fulfil that order the defendant required extra equipment which it ordered from the plaintiff; Point 3: lack of the equipment led to loss of the firm order and subsequent business with the third party, so the defendant no longer needed the extra equipment.

Cross-examine along the lines of the argument (see pages 96–100).

Example I:
Negligence—driving

Objectives:

(1) To get the plaintiff to accept that the layout of the road is as you describe—the bend is sharp and largely concealed

(2)   To get her to accept the collision was very near the stop-line
(3)   To establish that she is unfamiliar with this road. This, of course, has to be approached carefully, because her answer may be that she has used the road daily for years. But from her address and the evidence-in-chief as to her reason for the journey, there may be good reason carefully to explore the point
(4)   To put the defendant's case that the accident was caused by the plaintiff's clipping the bend

Example II:
Contract—debt

Objectives:

(1)   To get confirmation that the defendant notified the plaintiff the day after delivery that the wrong equipment had been delivered
(2)   To put the defendant's case that the equipment ordered was x, not y
(3)   To undermine the plaintiff's evidence as to what equipment was ordered
(4)   Nothing else needs to be put, challenged or elicited (because the rest of the defendant's argument rests on matters of which the plaintiff's witnesses have no knowledge)

Closing speeches

The defence speech is usually given before the plaintiff's (see pages 16–17). Give the judge, as briefly as possible, the reasons why s/he should find in your favour and illustrate the points by reference to the evidence.

Always address the judge argumentatively. Never quote the evidence except to illustrate a point you are making. Never directly ask the judge to take a specific view of a witness. Do it indirectly.

Example:
Not: "I submit the defendant gave his evidence very credibly."
But: "Your Honour may feel the defendant's evidence was supported on several points by the forensic evidence. The police accident report, for example, records that when the officers arrived, the defendant's car was just behind the stop-line ..."

The defence speech will generally take one of two forms. Very often the defence has set up a version of what happened different from the plaintiff's and may, of course, be pursuing a counterclaim. In that case, one is seeking to persuade the judge that the defence version is to be preferred (or theoretically that because the two versions are equally worthy of credit the plaintiff has not proved her/his case). The working plan and example of a prosecution speech (see pages 109–111) can be adapted.

Alternatively, the defence may be challenging only one part of the plaintiff's evidence and/or basing its defence on a point of law. In that case, the defence speech is more akin to the defence speech in a criminal case, in that all the fire is concentrated on one target.

There are two ways of structuring a speech on behalf of the plaintiff. One can answer point by point the argument on behalf of the defendant. The advantage of this approach is that it is seen to meet the defence case head-on. It also gives the impression that even when the defence choose the site of battle the plaintiff's case is stronger.

The alternative is to present one's argument that the plaintiff has made out her/his case without reference to the defence speech. The advantage of this is that the order of the points dealt with is more likely to be one advantageous to the plaintiff's case. It also avoids giving the impression that the structure of the defence speech indicates the correct way of approaching the dispute.

APPLICATION FOR SUMMARY JUDGMENT

Preparation

The following guide assumes you have had no involvement in the decision to apply for or resist summary judgment; or in drafting your client's affidavit.

Read the pleadings with an open mind. Briefly consider what evidence you would expect on both sides. Read the witness statements and correspondence. Make a chronology unless one has been provided.

Then read the applicant plaintiff's affidavit carefully, noting points in favour of, and against, her/his case. Check that the deponent has verified the facts and deposed that s/he believes there is no defence. Finally, read the respondent's affidavit, again noting points for and against. Does the evidence amount to a defence of the whole claim? If not, and you are acting for the defendant, you will need to take further instructions (see below).

Make three photocopies of any cases which you may want to draw to the district judge's attention. Calculate the interest on your claim to the hearing date.

Outside Chambers

Give copies of any cases to your opponent.

In Chambers

For the plaintiff applicant

Introduce your opponent to the district judge and in a sentence outline what you are seeking.

Example:
"May it please you, ma'am; I appear for the applicant, and my friend Mr Snubbin appears for the respondent. It is my application for summary judgment on part of the claim only."

Open the case as you would any other (see pages 72 to 74, and pages 169 to 171); be as economical as possible, but give the district judge all the information s/he needs. State briefly the nature of the claim and any counterclaim, and offer to read the Particulars of Claim.

Example:
"The plaintiff had supplied cattle feed to the defendant for several years until July of last year, and the defendant paid a monthly account. The last four payments have not been made.
"The defendant alleges that feed supplied in April and May was bad and caused sickness, which is the basis of the counterclaim. There is no complaint about the feed supplied in June and July and my application is for summary judgment on the price of that feed only.
"The Particulars of Claim were filed in February this year, and I wonder whether I can assist you, sir, by reading them?"

The district judge will either have already read the pleadings or will do so her/himself. Draw her/his attention to any important parts.

Example:
"I rely particularly, ma'am, on the second of the implied terms pleaded at paragraph 4."

Then offer to read the affidavit on behalf of the plaintiff. In the highly unlikely event that the district judge wishes the pleadings or affidavits to be read aloud, the defence advocate should read the defence pleadings and affidavits.

Arguments in favour of summary judgment fall into three categories. Firstly, that part of the claim is not defended (for example, of three alleged debts, the defence affidavit claims one was paid; the second is for goods which were not delivered; but the third is not mentioned at all).

Secondly, the defence is bad in law (for example, a tenant has refused to pay insurance premiums on the basis that that is the landlord's responsibility).

Thirdly, the defence is "shadowy".

For the second category of argument you may want to rely on case-law.

The third category of argument often depends upon the unusualness, even unnaturalness, of the defendant's behaviour and the number of coincidences in her/his account of events.

Your submissions are, in effect, a closing speech and as with any such submissions should not include wholesale repetition of the evidence, but deal with it lightly.

Example:

"...the admissions the defendant makes at paragraph 6, lines 7 and 12; and at paragraph 8, line 9..."

"...in my submission, the explanation the plaintiff gives, at paragraph 5, lines 9–22, is more consistent with the defendant's claim that the property was jointly owned, than with the plaintiff's contention ..."

As a general rule do not, at this stage, anticipate the defendant's arguments. You may well indicate points which had not occurred to your opponent, or put them more clearly.

When the defence advocate has made her/his submissions, reply as fully as you need to her/his arguments, but do not repeat any of your own points.

It is to some extent true that the more you argue you should have summary judgment, the less it appears you are entitled to it. It is a disposal suitable only for relatively clear cases.

For the respondent

If the affidavit on your client's behalf does not deal with the whole of the plaintiff's claim, you will need further instructions.

Example:

The plaintiff is claiming in nuisance for damage caused during building work done by your client and for a small trespass. Your client's affidavit disputes the nuisance but does not mention the trespass.

There are two possibilities. If, from the papers it is clear there is no defence to the relevant part of the claim, advise that you should be instructed to concede it. If there is a defence, it may be possible to prepare a brief supplemental affidavit before the hearing, otherwise you may be instructed to seek an adjournment.

If you have to accept that there is no defence to part of the claim, inform your opponent when you first meet. In the unlikely event that s/he does not mention the concession to the district judge, mention it youself as soon as your opponent has finished opening.

Example:
"May it please you, ma'am; I'm sorry to interrupt my friend, but it will assist you to know at this stage that the defendant accepts that there is no defence to the claim for payment of invoice number 420735 dated 11th July and therefore accepts the plaintiff is entitled to summary judgment on that part of the claim only, as I mentioned to my friend before we came into chambers."

Your arguments will fall into one or more of three categories. Firstly, that the plaintiff's claim is in some way bad in law. Secondly, and most commonly, that there is at least one triable issue of fact between the parties. Or thirdly, that although there may be little doubt that the plaintiff will win at trial, there is some good reason for a full hearing.

It is generally more effective to present your own arguments first before making any points in reply to your opponent's. In that way you first demonstrate there is more than one way of looking at the case and then show that the plaintiff's arguments are not so unassailable as they may have first appeared.

If summary judgment is awarded, apply for a stay of execution if you have been instructed that the defendant intends to appeal.

GLOSSARY

adjournment any postponement of case, whether for a few minutes (perhaps to allow advocate to take instructions) or several weeks

adjournment notice notice sent to defendant to inform her/him of date to which case has been adjourned

adjourn *sine die* adjourn indefinitely

admission a formal admission is the acceptance of a fact by a party in court, thereby obviating the need for proof. An informal admission is an out of court statement adverse to its maker

affirm of a witness, make a solemn declaration of the truth of the evidence s/he is about to give. An affirmation has the same legal status as an oath (*e.g.* untruthful evidence equally amounts to perjury). A religious believer who objects to taking an oath (perhaps at a particular time) is entitled to affirm

application to break an application made in open court to set aside a "fixture" (a pre-arranged hearing date)

arraignment the part of a Crown Court trial in which the clerk reads the counts on the indictment to the defendant who pleads "Guilty" or "Not Guilty" to each. It is in law the beginning of the trial (even if the trial is immediately adjourned to another date for a jury to be sworn)

assessed costs costs quantified by judge at the time of ordering payment

bail form the form given to a defendant when s/he is released on bail, informing her/him of the date when s/he must surrender to her/his bail (usually, the date of the next hearing)

bailiff a jury bailiff is an usher in the Crown Court who, pursuant to an oath taken in open court, ensures the privacy of the jury during its deliberations

bench warrant a warrant issued by the court for the arrest of a defendant who, having been released on bail, has failed to attend court. If it is "backed" for bail the police, after arresting the defendant, will release her/him on bail to attend on a new date. If it is not backed for bail, the police will keep the defendant in a cell until s/he can be brought to court

bill of indictment the draft indictment which becomes the indictment upon signature by the court officer

breaking a fixture the setting aside of a pre-arranged ("fixed") date for a County or Crown Court trial

certificate for counsel of an interlocutory county court hearing in chambers, a certificate issued by the judge (district or circuit) that counsel's attendance was appropriate. One is necessary only if the party's costs may be paid by the other side or by Legal Aid

conditional bail bail granted subject to restrictions on the defendant's liberty ("conditions") which the magistrate decides. If the defendant cannot meet the conditions (*e.g.* find a surety) s/he remains in prison

costs in the cause of an interlocutory hearing, the costs will be paid by the party which ultimately loses the action

costs on scale 1 (2, etc.) a basis of taxation of costs whereby greater amounts are allowed the higher the scale, the scale being determined by the value of the action

costs reserved of an interlocutory hearing, each party must bear its own costs unless a contrary order is made at the final hearing of the action

costs to be assessed costs to be quantified by the judge at the time of ordering payment

draft indictment also called the "bill of indictment", a document listing the charges against a defendant which, upon signature by the court officer, becomes the indictment

dressing the court the convention that at least one advocate remains in court whenever a tribunal of law is present, unless released with the words, "Please don't wait"

either-way offence one which, in the case of an adult, may be tried either in the Crown or magistrates' court, and for which, therefore, there must be Mode of Trial proceedings

effective of a case, ready for immediate trial. An "effective date" is a date set for trial, *cf* a "non-effective" date, for which witnesses will not be warned

empannelled empannelling is the process of choosing and swearing a jury

endorse/endorsement writing on an advocate's instructions by the advocate (to record proceedings at hearing); or the lay client (to authorise a course of action)

estreat of a recognisance, confiscate. If a defendant fails to answer her/his bail, the court may deprive any surety of the sum of money pledged (the "recognisance")

execution of a warrant for arrest, the arrest of the person named

finding a decision on fact by a tribunal

first instance first coming. (i) a court of first instance is one in which a matter is tried for the first time *cf* appellate court; (ii) a warrant at first instance is one issued pursuant to section 13 of the Magistrates' Courts Act 1980 to compel an unconvicted defendant who is not on bail, to attend. It may be backed for bail, or not *cf* bench warrant

fixture   a hearing in the County or Crown Court for which the date is set in advance

floater   in the Crown Court, a case which has not been fixed for a specific time, but is put into a "warned" list of cases which may be called any time in a two-week period. One afternoon, parties are notified the case will be one of several "floaters" the next day. The floaters are called on as courts become free

form   previous convictions

form MG16   list of previous convictions

form 609   former name of form MG16

formal admission   an acceptance of a fact by a party in court, thereby obviating the need for proof *cf* informal admission

go over   of case, be adjourned (whether to the afternoon, or to another date)

half-time submission   submission of no case to answer made at the close of plaintiff's or prosecution case

indemnity costs   a basis of taxation of costs on which any doubt as to reasonableness of amount is resolved in favour of the receiving party, contrary to the general rule

indictable   an offence which, in the case of an adult, may be tried in the Crown Court (whether or not it may also be tried in the magistrates' court), *cf* indictable only

indictable only   an offence which, in the case of an adult, can be tried only in the Crown Court

indictment   in Crown Court proceedings, the document containing the charges to which the defendant is asked to plead "Guilty" or "Not Guilty"

informal admission   an out of court statement adverse to its maker *cf* formal admission

information   (i) an allegation made, orally or in writing, to a magistrates' court, in response to which the court issues a summons to the defendant to attend court; (ii) the written charge(s) to which the defendant is asked to plead "Guilty" or "Not Guilty" at the beginning of a summary trial

in session   of a magistrates' court, sitting

instance, at first   *see* first instance

instructions   the authority of a client to a lawyer to act for her/him in legal proceedings. It is important to have these in writing, so that both sides are clear as to the extent of the lawyer's authority (for example, in negotiation)

IRB police officer's Incident Report Book

jury bailiff an usher in the Crown Court who, pursuant to an oath taken in open court, ensures the privacy of the jury during its deliberations

list in the magistrates' court, the cases allocated to a particular court-room for that morning or afternoon

loser's statement the evidence (usually served and accepted section 9) of a victim of crime who has lost, or had damaged, property (by theft, burglary, taking a conveyance, etc.)

"no case" submission of no case to answer made at the close of plaintiff's or prosecution case

non-effective of a case, not ready for immediate trial. Of a date, one on which it is not intended trial will take place, so witnesses will not be warned

non-suit of a plaintiff in the county court, termination of trial without judgment being given for either party

oral information in the magistrates' court, an allegation made orally that a person has committed a criminal offence. In response to the information the court issues a summons to that person to attend court, or, if the person is already a defendant to other charges (*e.g.* if the oral information relates to a Bail Act offence in subsisting proceedings) adds the new charge to the existing ones

original the original, usually hand-written, signed statement of a witness. If the evidence is read section 9, the original is handed in to the court (at the hearing, in the magistrates' court; at transfer, in the Crown Court). When a witness gives oral evidence, the party calling her/him should have the original to hand in case the other party wishes it to be shown to the witness (*e.g.* to demonstrate inconsistency)

previous previous convictions

put over of a case, be adjourned (whether to the afternoon or another date)

quoshed of a conviction or sentence, nullified. "Squashed" is a mis-hearing

recognisance *see* surety

remand of a criminal case, a hearing prior to the case being set for trial; of a list ("the remand list"), a list of remand cases (or "remands") set for hearing in the same courtroom; of a defendant, is of three kinds, all of which are restrictions on the defendant's liberty during the period between first appearance in court and final disposal of the case: (i) "remand in custody"; (ii) (of youths only) "remand into local authority accommodation" (iii) "remand on conditional/unconditional bail. If the defendant is unable to meet the conditions of her/his bail (*e.g.* is unable to find a surety), s/he remains in prison. Remand on unconditional bail is the least onerous, the only restriction being the duty to surrender to the court's custody at a specified time

reporting   a condition of bail requiring the defendant to "report to" or "sign on at" a named police station at specified times each week, to lessen the risk of absconding

residence   a condition of bail requiring the defendant to live and sleep every night at a named address (usually her/his home)

retire/retiring   of a tribunal of law, to leave the courtroom (*e.g.* to deliberate a verdict or other decision)

rise/rising   of a tribunal of law, to leave the courtroom (*e.g.* to deliberate a verdict or other decision)

section nine   the provision of the Criminal Justice Act 1967 pursuant to which a party to criminal proceedings may serve on the other party at least seven days before trial a statement of evidence prefixed with a declaration as to its truth, which, in the absence of prior written objection by the other party, the party may read without calling the statement's maker

seised   a variant of "seized"; of a court, aware or informed of

serious enough   of a crime, warranting a community sentence (Criminal Justice Act 1991, section 6(1))

session   in the magistrates' court, the total of the cases allocated to a particular courtroom for a given morning or afternoon

signing on   a condition of bail requiring the defendant to "sign on at" or "report to" a named police station at specified times each week, to lessen the risk of absconding

sine die   "without day"; indefinitely

six-o-nine ("609")   former name of form MG16

squashed   of a conviction, a mishearing of "quoshed"

so serious   of a crime, one for which only a custodial sentence can be justified (Criminal Justice Act 1991, section 1(2)(a))

stand out/stood out   of a case, adjourned (whether for a few minutes or a few weeks)

stipendiary   a legally-qualified, paid magistrate who may sit alone

submission   a proposition, whether of fact, law or mixed fact and law, put forward by an advocate for consideration or ruling by a tribunal. Each submission will not necessarily be ruled upon separately or at all. Every speech is, if effect, a series of submissions

summary   of jurisdiction, the jurisdiction of the magistrates' court; of offence, one triable only in the magistrates' court; of trial, trial in a magistrates' court

summons in the magistrates' court, a document issued by a the court inviting the defendant to attend the hearing of an allegation against her/him (attendance, despite the name, is not compulsory)

surety in criminal proceedings, a person who undertakes to ensure the attendance of a defendant at court, in default of which s/he will lose a sum of money (the "recognisance"). The surety may be taken (s/he may "enter into her/his recognisance") in court or at a police station. The police may object to her/his suitability. It is an offence to agree to indemnify a surety against her/his liability

surrender of a defendant on bail, attendance when required at court and subjection of her/himself to the court's directions

sworn a jury is sworn when each member has taken the jury oath

taking instructions conferring between advocate and client in which advocate advises client and client indicates her/his decision, or provides information

tender make available for cross-examination by an opposing party a witness whom a party has brought to court, but then decided not to examine (see page 90)

tribunal decider. May be of facts, law, or both. In the Crown Court, the judge as the tribunal of law rules on legal points; the jury as tribunal of fact decides the facts; in most civil matters the judge is the tribunal of law and fact; and magistrates are always tribunals of both law and fact

unconditional bail bail, of which the only condition is an obligation to surrender to a named court or police station at a specified time

vacate of a trial date, set aside

warned list in the Crown Court, a list of cases which may be heard on any day within a two-week period, the parties being notified the evening before. These "floating cases" ("floaters") are called on as courts become free

warrant *see* bench warrant; first instance warrant

INDEX